CANADIAN DOLLARS & SENSE

Building a Budget

IN THIS BOOK

- Assess your spending and learn which expenses are essential and which are nonessential
- Create a budget that puts you on track to a secure financial future — and stick to it
- Get yourself out of debt and develop a savings program
- Revise and update your goals as your circumstances change

John Wiley & Sons Canada, Ltd.

Library and Archives Canada Cataloguing in Publication Data

Building a budget.
(Canadian dollars & sense)

ISBN 978-1-11-801374-8

1. Budgets, Personal. 2. Finance, Personal. I. Series: Canadian dollars & sense

HG179.B85 2010   332.024   C2010-906520-4

This publication is designed to provide accurate and authoritative information in regard to the subject matter covered. It is sold on the understanding that the Publisher is not engaged in rendering professional services. If professional advice or other expert assistance is required, the services of a competent professional should be sought.

Production Credits
Cover design: Ian Koo and Adrian So
Interior design and typesetting: Adrian So and Natalia Burobina
Cover image: © Thinkstock/Comstock
Printer: Printcrafters

John Wiley & Sons Canada, Ltd.
6045 Freemont Blvd.
Mississauga, Ontario
L5R 4J3

Printed in Canada

1 2 3 4 5 PC 15 14 13 12 11

table of contents

introduction

Because you picked up this book, we know that you're at least somewhat motivated to start living on a budget so that you can take control of your spending and start saving. You've come to the right place! *Building a Budget* takes a practical look at many phases of creating a budget. You'll find information that you can use to pursue better management of your money so that it can go further and lead to investments that will provide greater financial security.

Why Do You Need This Book?

Can you answer yes to any of these questions?

- Do you need to learn about creating a budget fast?
- Do you not have the time to read 500 pages on budgeting?
- Do you find that you don't know where your money goes?

- Do you want to be able to meet your financial goals and have a secure financial future?

Then *Building a Budget* is for you!

How to Use This Book

How to use this book is really up to you — you need to find the approach that works best for your own situation. The important thing is to get started. Unless you do something to take control of your money, nothing will happen.

Here are some ways that we recommend you search for the information you need:

- Flip through the book and look for the topic in the running head across the top of each page.
- Check the table of contents at the front of the book.
- Look through the topic list at the beginning of each chapter.
- Flip through the book until you find what you need — the book is organized in a logical, task-oriented way.

For additional sources of information about money management, check the Resource Centre at the back of the book.

CHAPTER 1

"you are here" in your financial life

IN THIS CHAPTER

- Figuring out what you're worth
- Looking at your goals
- Setting your timeline for reaching those goals

Whether you're in Montreal, Medicine Hat, or Mozambique, every map you come across will have a "You Are Here" arrow. Why? Because you can't get where you want to go if you don't know where you are.

Your budget is a financial map to help you reach your financial goals. Determine your current financial situation by taking a thorough survey of your current financial status. This chapter shows you how.

Committing time to build your financial plan may be your most important investment in your future.

Figuring Out What You're Worth

When budgeting, people usually think of "worth" as cash in the form of salary, savings, chequing accounts, and so on. But you can make a number of decisions about anything you have that has value. Did you inherit a really ugly — but valuable (to someone else!) — vase from Uncle Ted? Save your memories; sell the vase.

Income

How much money do you take home after federal, provincial, and municipal taxes; and pension, unemployment insurance, and health benefit deductions? (Most people budget on a monthly basis, but if you get paid weekly or semimonthly, you may want your budget to reflect that income pattern.)

You may wish to include temporary, part-time, or seasonal income. On the other hand, you might choose to treat that extra income like "found money" and put it directly into your savings or investment plan. With the benefits of compound interest, such microinvestments may mean much to your future. We discuss *compounding* (interest that is paid on interest already earned) later in the book so that you truly understand the benefits of forgoing small pleasures now for giant rewards.

Savings

How much money do you have in your bank, trust, or credit union savings account(s)? Do you have a money market account? Guaranteed Investment Certificates (GICs)? For the purposes of figuring out your financial worth, your savings list includes *liquid assets*, or assets that you can readily turn into cash. (If you find that you have too many accounts in too many places, try consolidating them into fewer accounts. By consolidating, you can save fees, make tracking your assets easier, and make more money with accounts that pay higher interest.)

Other assets

The "other assets" category itemizes your less-liquid holdings. Some may not figure into your monthly budget, but you need to be aware of them. By evaluating these assets carefully, you may find that you can make them serve your purposes better by liquidating them (converting them into cash) and applying their value in another category.

Other assets include stocks; bonds; mutual funds; retirement funds; insurance; real estate; and other investments, such as vehicles (land, water, *or* air!), jewellery, cash value of insurance policies, and collectibles (like stamps or antiques).

Calculate your net worth using the following worksheet:

My Net Worth as of

Cash

Chequing account(s)   _____

Savings account(s)   _____

Money market account(s)   _____

GICs   _____

Other   _____

Stocks, Bonds, and Mutual Funds

Stocks   _____

Bonds   _____

Mutual funds   _____

Commodities   _____

Securities   _____

Options   _____

Other   _____

Building a Budget

Retirement Funds
RRSP(s) or RRIF(s) _____

TFSA _____

Company pension plan _____

Profit-sharing plan _____

Other _____

Real Estate
Equity in main residence _____

Equity in vacation home(s) _____

Equity in co-owned property _____

Equity in rental property _____

Other _____

Insurance
Annuities, surrender value of _____

Life insurance, cash value of _____

Personal Property
Airplane(s) _____

Antique(s) _____

Art: painting(s), sculpture(s), etc. _____

Automobile(s) _____

Boat(s) _____

Camper(s) _____

Collectibles: stamps, coins, etc. _____

Gold and/or silver _____

Household
Furniture, appliances, etc. _____

Jewellery	
Recreational vehicle(s)	
Other	

As you remember other assets, return to this worksheet and enter the values.

Setting Your Goals

One reason that some individuals and families find it hard to set goals is that generally people are not good at looking at saving money in terms of long timelines. We don't even look at debt in terms of long timelines. When you buy something that you don't really need because it will cost "only" $30 a month, you're ignoring how much the total cost, including interest, will be.

When you think about savings, you may see saving $30 a month as an awfully slow way to accumulate assets because you ignore interest compounding (discussed at the end of this chapter). Saving is like the woman who, at age 47, hesitated to start medical school because she would be 51 by the time she got her degree. She finally decided to pursue her dream when her counsellor pointed out that she would be 51 in four years, whether or not she went back to school.

Setting goals is more than just writing down a dollar amount. It's a way to ensure that you will not only enjoy your dreams, but also the pursuit itself and the steps you take forward along the way.

Goals are usually divided into short-term, mid-term, and long-term goals. These terms mean different things to each budget planner, depending on where you are on your life's path.

At the start of 2010, the average life expectancy in Canada was 80 years, up almost 68 percent since the turn of the 20th century.

During your lifetime, what you *want* — and what you *need* — are different at each stage of your life. Meeting goals in the short term not only reinforces that you can meet your longer-term goals but also (happily) reinforces your determination to do so.

Budgeting is not denying yourself pleasures and happiness. Rather, it is creating a financial plan that not only will allow, but ensure, that you'll have a joyful life at every age. Consider, for example, your addiction to non-fat chai lattes. If you spend $4 to $10 a day for 48 weeks a year, that little pleasure will cost you $1,344 to $3,360 a year. Add an expensive gourmet pastry to that, and the amount could double. Close your eyes and remember: five minutes after drinking either that chai latte or the teabag-in-a-cup version you slug back for free at work, can you really recall what either tasted like? Get something memorable for your money!

Budgets don't cause stress; the *lack* of a budget causes stress.

Short-term goals

You can set short-terms goals for as soon as next week or as long as a year. The good news is that the dollar amount you need to have to meet these goals will not grow appreciably due to inflation. The bad news is that the "free" money you'll add to your fund from interest payments will be less than for longer-term goals.

Short-term goals may include paying for a vacation, buying a new sound system, or being able to attend your brother's wedding on the other side of the country.

Short-term goals may be "stepping stones" on the way to longer-term goals, such as accumulating a down payment for a home or car or starting a child's college or university fund. In Table 1-1, fill in your own short-term goals and the dates by which you wish to achieve them. (The first three items are examples to help get you started.)

Table 1-1: My Short-Term Goals

Goal	Goal Date
1. Save for car down payment	
2. Start house fund	
3. Save for share of parents' anniversary party	
4.	
5.	
6.	
7.	
8.	

Mid-term goals

Mid-term goals are one-year to five-year plans. Both the negative effects of inflation and the positive effects of compounding interest will be greater in these goals than in your short-term goals.

Mid-term goals might include a down payment on a vacation home or boat, going back to school, and meeting your first-through fifth-year goals on your way to meeting your long-term retirement fund goals. In Table 1.2, fill in your own mid-term goals and the dates by which you hope to achieve them.

Table 1-2: My Mid-Term Goals

Goal	Goal Date
1.	
2.	
3.	
4.	
5.	
6.	
7.	
8.	

Long-term goals

Your long-term goals are five-year or longer plans. For long-term plans like retirement, you will have goals within that time frame. For example, your retirement savings plans may include goals for 5, 10, 15, or 20 years.

As you meet each goal, your resolve to meet your other goals will be firmer. But, as with the rest of life, your goals themselves may need to be updated. Changes in the goals of individual family members may necessitate revising the family goals. Career changes, health factors, and responsibility for extended family members are some reasons your long-term goals may need revising. On the other hand, winning the lottery might change your timeline on some goals!

All news that affects your financial picture — good or not-so-good news — means going back to your financial road map to see whether you're still heading toward your goals.

In Table 1-3, fill in your own long-term goals and the dates by which you hope to achieve them.

Table 1-3: My Long-Term Goals

Goal	Goal Date
1.	
2.	
3.	
4.	
5.	
6.	
7.	
8.	

Determining How Much Your Goals Will Cost

For each goal, and according to its particular time frame, the following questions can help you decide how much you need to save to meet that goal:

- How much would this goal cost if you were to buy/pay for it today?
- Using an appropriate rate of inflation, how much is the goal likely to cost on its due date?
- Using historical rates of inflation, you can calculate the average rate, and then apply it over the term of reaching a goal. This tells you what the total cost is likely to be, taking into account rising prices.
- If your goal has its own inflation rate — for example, the cost of education is rising at a faster rate than overall inflation — use that rate.
- What average after-tax rate of interest do you expect to earn on your savings for this goal?
- How much will compounding your earned interest add to your savings for this goal?

Base your calculations on the highest estimated costs. That way, you won't be caught short. You can always transfer the "extra" to your own retirement plan. To figure out how much your estimated savings will increase over time, go to moneycentral. msn.com and search for the handy "savings calculator."

Evelyn had always spent her money wisely, but she wasn't as good at saving. Her financial planner, Betty, went through her expenses and convinced Evelyn that she could save $50 a month without making any real sacrifice.

"Fine," Evelyn acquiesced, "but that's not enough money to make a real difference in my future financial security."

"No?" challenged Betty. "Look at this table showing how you can grow that little investment into a major asset."

If you saved $50 per month, compounding would increase your investment to the amounts listed in Table 1-4.

Table 1-4: The Impact of Compounding Interest

Year	At 0%	At 3%	At 4%
5	$3,000	$3,232	$3,315
10	$6,000	$6,987	$7,362
15	$9,000	$11,349	$12,305
20	$12,000	$16,415	$18,339
25	$15,000	$22,300	$25,706
30	$18,000	$29,137	$34,702
35	$21,000	$37,078	$45,687
40	$24,000	$46,303	$59,098
45	$27,000	$57,019	$75,473
50	$30,000	$69,466	$95,468

Notice the difference that even 1 percent interest makes in the accumulation of dollars. If you add some stocks to your investment plan, you should be able to count on a higher rate of return over time. Evelyn started her savings plan immediately. So should you!

CHAPTER 2

looking at where your money goes

IN THIS CHAPTER

- Evaluating your spending habits
- Putting your spending into categories
- Learning about the tools for tracking your spending
- Identifying how you think about money and spending

In your financial life, you may be spending (or paying bills) until you have no more money. Then you wait for payday and start the process all over again. That approach may have worked (although not all that well) back in the days when you were collecting an allowance from Mom and Dad. It may have worked even in university — at least you wouldn't freeze. As time goes on, though, this "system" becomes less and less sound.

This chapter helps you figure out where you are currently spending your money so that you can lay the groundwork to set up your budget. A budget enables you to make wiser, more informed decisions about your spending.

Keeping a Spending Diary

Keeping a spending diary helps you determine how you're spending your money on a day-to-day basis. For your diary, use a small notebook that fits in your pocket or purse. Carry it everywhere. Attach a pen or pencil to it so you have no excuse for not writing down every purchase you make. Every day. Every cent. Keep your spending diary for at least a month.

On each new page, write the day and date. Record your purchases whether you spent cash, used a credit card, or added to a tab. At the end of each day, total your expenses. (To make this exercise even more useful, divide your weekly after-tax income by seven, write that amount on each day's page, and at the end of the day figure out whether you spent more than you made that day.)

There are three ways to keep your diary:

- Use two columns: one for the amount and one for a description.
- Decide how many categories you want, and then draw and label your columns (you'll probably use two facing pages). Categories might include groceries, restaurant meals, snacks, transportation, clothing, and telephone calls.
- Draw fewer columns for wider categories, such as food, transportation, utilities, clothes, and miscellaneous. Write a key in the front or back of your notebook so that you can keep track of the items within each category. For example, under food you could use G for groceries, R for restaurant meals, S for snacks, and so on, as shown in Table 2-1.

Table 2-1: My Spending Diary for [Today's Date]

Food	Transportation	Miscellaneous
R $12.00	B $5.25	C $39.00
S $3.50	F $39.48	T $2.75
G $66.88		

If your miscellaneous column adds up too fast, you probably need more categories. And if you find that you're altering your spending habits as you keep your diary, don't write your totals until the end of the month.

Using Other Tools to Track Your Spending

Did you realize that your bank and credit card statements can help you create a budget? Rather than just checking to make sure that the amounts are correct, use these records to see how much money you spend in each category. Use the same key that you used earlier for your spending diary.

Using the information that you've gathered, you put pencil to paper to create a budgeting worksheet. Financial software has long been inexpensive and easy to use; it's another good way to keep track of your spending and saving habits.

The time you invest now to gather your information and set up your budget pays off in easier tracking and decision making later. You've already made the decisions about your money; now you just have to apply them.

Bank records

Banking online makes it easy to reconcile your bank statements with your spending. You can see current and even past records on the Internet. You can find out whether a specific cheque has cleared and check your current balance. You can go over your records when it's convenient for you rather than waiting for the post office to deliver your statement.

If you still prefer to use paper records, pay close attention to the monthly statement that your bank, credit union, or other financial institution sends you. Use different-coloured highlighters to put your expenditures in categories: To start, try green for savings and red for impulse purchases.

The easier you make it to keep track of your finances, the more likely you are to do it. Remember that all these bills can be paid automatically, if you're not doing this already:

- Mortgage
- Utilities
- Land line and cellphones
- Credit cards
- Savings

Credit card statements

Those handy reports that you get every month recording your credit card activity also help you draw your financial map. Whipping out the card to make a purchase is so easy that many people do so much more often than they should. Again, using highlighters, mark each purchase to be tallied in a specific category.

Budgeting software

Programs like Quicken are inexpensive yet flexible. These programs do the basics, like keeping track of your cheque record and balancing your chequebook. But that's just the beginning.

Like the paper worksheet in Table 2-2, later in this chapter, budgeting software creates a budget for you according to your specifications. Even better than automatically calculating totals as you enter amounts, the software enables you to move items from category to category. (For example, you may want to move restaurant meals from the Food to the Personal category.) You can also create what Quicken calls supergroups. For example, you can put housing, transportation, and food under a supergroup called "basic."

Why are supergroups important? Because you don't have to add up the same group totals repeatedly. On the other hand, you still have the total for smaller groups without having to separate and add them up one by one.

Flexibility allows you to reorganize your budget so that it gives you the information you want. Once you've set up a budget, you aren't stuck with it. And as your situation changes, you can customize your budget to reflect your new reality.

Depending on the software package you buy, you can compare your forecasted spending with actual spending in any category, know when expenses are due with the use of a financial calendar, monitor your loan payments, manage your investments, and create reports and graphs to show how you're progressing toward your goals.

Don't put off budgeting because you don't have a computer. Software is nice, but not necessary.

If you have a friend or family member who is an expert in one software package, buy it! You'll have your own software coach.

Evaluating Where Your Money Goes

With your spending diary in hand, you have the information you need to set up your budget. Knowing where your money goes can help you keep it from going.

Table 2-2 is a budgeting worksheet that shows you what your history of spending looks like. Using the last six months of bank and credit card records, figure your expenses in each category. For items that fluctuate, like food, add up your six-month total (SMT). Then double that amount to get your yearly cost. Divide your SMT by two for your quarterly cost for that item. Divide your SMT by six to determine your monthly cost. Divide your SMT by 26 to calculate your weekly cost. Prepare to be shocked at how much you're spending in some categories.

Table 2-2: My Budget Worksheet

Expenses	Weekly	Monthly	Yearly
Housing			
Rent or mortgage			
Condo association dues			
Maintenance			
Property taxes			
Insurance			
Furniture and appliances			
Other			
Utilities			
Gas			
Telephone – home and mobile			
Water			
Electricity			
Food			
Groceries			
Eating out			
Other			
Transportation			
Automobile lease/payment 1			
Automobile lease/payment 2			
Licensing			

Expenses	Weekly	Monthly	Yearly
Insurance			
Maintenance			
Gasoline			
Taxis and public transportation			
Parking/tolls			
Other			
Health			
Chiropractor(s)			
Dentist(s)			
Eye care			
Prescriptions			
Insurance			
Other			
Education			
Tuition/school fees			
Books and supplies			
School activities			
Other			
Personal			
Clothing, shoes			
Haircuts			
Cosmetics			
Pet care			
Childcare			
Child support (you pay out)			
Allowances			
Gifts			
Donations			
Membership dues			

continued

Building a Budget

Expenses	Weekly	Monthly	Yearly
Magazines, books, and newspaper subscriptions			
Laundry/dry cleaning			
Hobbies			
Vacations			
Entertainment			
Other			
Savings and Investment Contributions			
Savings accounts			
RRSP(s)			
Tax-Free Savings Account (TFSA)			
Mutual funds			
Bonds			
Other			
Credit and Loan Payments			
Credit card 1			
Credit card 2			
Credit card 3			
Department store card			
Gasoline card			
Student loan			
Other			
TOTAL EXPENSES			
Income			
Wages, total			
Gratuities			
Royalties			
Dividends and interest			
Trust fund			
Pension			

Expenses	Weekly	Monthly	Yearly
CPP and EI			
Child support paid to you			
Gifts			
TOTAL INCOME			

You can add, subtract, or rearrange items to create a worksheet that fits your particular situation.

Now you know how much you're spending in each category. After you create a budget based on what you *want* to spend in each category and adjust your spending habits accordingly, you'll be able to tell when you overspend or underspend in a category. Neither situation is cause for despair or jubilation as long as your long-term expenditures stay within your personal range. If you consistently overspend, you may need to cut costs, or you may have underestimated your costs initially. On the other hand, if you consistently underspend your allowance in any category, you may be able to lower that budget item and reallocate the difference.

Identifying Your Money Personality

The best-laid plans are worthless if you can't follow them. To find the best plans for *you*, and to help yourself stick to your budget, you need to understand how you feel about money and how you react to money matters. Figure out which of the following money personality types most accurately describes you:

- **Saver:** You have trouble spending money even when doing so is in your best interests.
- **Spender:** Your immediate reaction to available cash (or even available credit) is to figure out what you can buy with it. Sometimes you spend because you can't resist salespeople.

Spenders use credit if they don't have cash, with no concern for the long-term consequences of that debt.

- **Impulse buyer:** When you see something you like, you buy it without evaluating the purchase in terms of your long-range goals. Impulse buyers react to one or two types of items (whereas spenders buy everything!).
- **Cautious buyer:** You are a serious comparison shopper who may waste more time making a decision than the item is worth.

You need to understand not only your own money personality, but that of your spouse or partner as well. (As you teach your children about budgeting and saving, you'll need to identify their money personalities, too.) Once you recognize your money personality type, you can identify what habits you need to keep or change to reach your financial goals:

- You might think that a saver wouldn't have any changes to make. But you can actually save to the point of hurting yourself.

For example, when Dorothy moved in with her mother, seven people from her workplace volunteered to help her move. Her new home was a three-hour round-trip drive from her old home. The truck rental contract called for a forfeit of the $45 deposit if the truck wasn't returned by 2 p.m., but included no added hourly rental charge as long as the truck was returned by 5 p.m.

So with seven no-cost workers, Dorothy hurriedly loaded the truck, left everything in the unattached garage at her mother's home, and rushed back before the 2 p.m. deadline. Yes, she saved

$45. But she left many expensive things stored in a garage without climate control. In addition, two of her "workers" were no-longer-young women — one 82 and the other 56 — who had to move heavy furniture up stairs to get it into the house.

Did Dorothy "save"?

- A spender has more problems to overcome than the obvious. The attitude that any money available is available only to spend, rather than to put in savings, is its own problem. But it's not unbeatable. If you learn to stop, evaluate, consider alternatives, and make a decision instead of reacting to the desire to spend (or giving in to a sales pitch), you'll have a more secure financial future.
- An impulse spender is similar to a spender. But an impulse spender doesn't even have to "find" money available for spending. Just seeing something to buy is enough to bring out the wallet or credit card. The desirable habit to cultivate is the same as that for a spender. If you figure how many hours of after-tax income would be needed to buy an item, you can stop much of your impulse buying in its tracks. If you have a working sound system, for example, is it really worth hundreds of work hours to replace it with a new one?
- Cautious buyers may waste both time and money. But time *is* money. Not only may a cautious buyer spend too much time gathering information about various features and comparing prices, but there's also the cost of phone calls and driving around. Even worse, a cautious buyer may not enjoy a purchase after making it if he or she sees the item on sale later. If you're a cautious buyer, use those good comparison-buying skills, but learn when enough information is enough

to make a decision, and ignore any information that you gather after the purchase. If you have a lot of trouble making a buying decision, you may not need to buy that item at all.

CHAPTER 3

creating a budget

IN THIS CHAPTER

- Learning techniques to recognize *all* your expenses
- Categorizing your spending into essentials and nonessentials
- Recognizing that you have money available to start saving

In Chapters 1 and 2, you gathered and organized information so that you can create a realistic and workable budget. In this chapter, you'll use the information that you collected, making changes and fine-tuning so your tools will work for you.

Determining Your Essential Expenses: What You Need

Essential fixed expenses are those obligations that you must pay regularly — usually monthly. Essential fixed expenses are the same month after month.

Essential variable expenses are due every month, but the amounts vary from month to month: food, gas, electricity, long-distance telephone expenses, and so on. In this category, you *prorate* (that is, you average) regular expenses to calculate your monthly cost. Do so by figuring your yearly cost and dividing by 12 (if you're using a monthly budget) or 52 (if you're using a weekly budget).

Essential fixed expenses include:

- Insurance that you pay quarterly, semiannually, or annually
- Mortgage payment or rent
- Automobile payment
- Student loan payment

Essential variable expenses include:

- Groceries
- Utilities (gas, electricity, water, and so on)
- Public transit fares
- Gasoline
- Auto repairs and maintenance
- Health care
- Education costs (for your children or yourself)
- Haircuts, toiletries, and other personal care items
- Savings for retirement
- Savings for large expenses, such as furniture, appliances, and replacement automobiles

Although charitable contributions generally are not considered essential expenses, you can put those items in the essential category if you want to pay them regularly.

As you update your budget, you'll remove items such as student loans as you pay them off.

Determining Your Nonessential Expenses: What You Want

After you pay your essential expenses, what you have left is your *discretionary income*. From that, you pay your nonessential expenses (and put the rest in savings and investments).

Nonessential expenses include the following:

- Books, magazines, and newspaper subscriptions
- Restaurant meals
- Movies and concerts
- Gifts
- Vacations
- Hobbies

Chapter 2 lists various money personalities. These personalities identify how you feel about money and spending. Recognizing your money personality — and the money personalities of family members — helps you make better decisions about the money that you've identified as nonessential spending.

In Table 2-1 back in Chapter 2, you discovered where your money went in the past. In creating your budget, you're looking toward the future. You want to determine which items that you listed as fixed expenses really should be considered nonessential. You may be shocked at the total of these items, but don't be discouraged. You'll learn how to reduce expenses in Chapter 5.

The whole point of a budget is to have a plan for your money before you spend it. Without a budget, you can leave the house with $200 in cash, come back five hours later, and be able to account for only half that amount. With a budget, you'll never do that again. More important, you will be able to make firm spending decisions based on criteria that you have already set for yourself.

Recognizing and Avoiding Hidden Expenses

Hidden expenses are those sneaky money-eaters that lurk everywhere. Knowing what and where they are and how much they cost helps you reduce or eliminate them.

This section identifies hidden costs. Chapter 5 shows you how to cut them.

Bank machine, bank, and credit card fees

Hidden costs can quickly transfer your money from your pocket to an institution's profit statement. Be careful of the following:

- Annual fees
- Below-minimum use and below-minimum balance fees
- High interest rates
- Late-payment penalties
- Per-use fees

Read all "change of terms" inserts that you receive from banks, credit unions, credit card companies, and the like. The information that they contain may be a call to change how and where you do business.

Not knowing what fees you're liable for with your money-handling institutions is the same as using a credit card without knowing the interest rate. If you don't carry a balance on your credit card, the interest rate is irrelevant. If you don't incur fees from your bank and so on, you don't care what that rate is, either. But you need to know what and how much they are so that you know what to do to avoid them.

Gratuities and delivery charges

The more services you use in your lifestyle, the more you'll pay in gratuities and delivery charges. Having meals or groceries delivered is convenient and may save you time, but in addition to paying for what you eat, you pay delivery costs and a tip to the delivery person — neither of which you can have for dessert.

Catalogue and Internet shopping can save a lot of time, along with parking and car-use costs. An add-on cost, however, may be shipping charges (often unrecoverable if you return the item). You may need to pay insurance costs to protect against the item getting lost or damaged in transit, and if you're purchasing from the U.S. there may be customs charges as well. Keep in mind that, when you buy something in a store, you can inspect it before you take it home.

This doesn't mean that you should always shop in stores; it just means that you need to know and compare the costs of various ways of taking care of your needs. If you use the time you save to earn more income, for example, the convenience may be worth the cost.

Sales, luxury, and utility taxes

Not all items are taxed at the same rate. Basic groceries, for example, are not taxed anywhere in Canada, but "snacks" (basically anything that can be eaten in one sitting) are, in some jurisdictions.

Governments have determined some items as luxury items. Liquor is a common example. In some places, the tax on a soft drink is lower than the tax on a beer — even though you drink either one. The choices you make in what may seem to be the same category can lower these hidden costs. Read your receipts carefully. Some cash registers put added taxes next to the item purchased so that you can readily see how much you're paying for items for which substitutes may be available.

Choosing one item over another may not save you a ton of money, but making saving decisions over and over can help put you on the path to financial security.

Factoring in Emergency Expenses

You don't want to panic every time the refrigerator breaks down or the dog eats spoiled food and has to go to the vet. Whether or not such items appeared in your assessment of your spending in Chapter 2 (see Table 2-2), emergencies will happen. That worksheet reflects what you spent in the past. The budget you'll create later in this chapter reflects that emergencies do happen, so you'll have the savings put aside to pay for such contingencies.

You can move some items from the emergency category to a "savings for replacement" category by keeping track of those budget items. For example, one of the biggest money-eaters in the emergency category can be your vehicle, especially if it isn't maintained properly and regularly.

Table 3-1 can help you keep track of your car's care and feeding. List all repairs, regular service (whether done at a service station or by you), and tire purchases. Review your car's service manual to be certain that you're following the manufacturer's recommendations.

Table 3-1: Auto Maintenance: Major Repairs

Date	Odometer Reading	Repair Description	Repair Warranty	Cost	Date Last Done

When deciding which auto parts to buy, the existence of a warranty and its terms can be deciding factors. Keeping track of the life of the warranty helps you get your money's worth. If a shop wants to add chargeable parts or labour to those covered by the warranty, ask to see what needs to be replaced and why.

Some warranties are prorated (the cost for wear and tear is deducted), and others offer replacements (you get a new tire or other part). Knowing what you're buying makes comparisons easier.

Keep similar records on major appliances and furniture. Table 3-2 shows you what information you need to plan replacement purchases.

Table 3-2: Major Purchases/Replacement Needs

Item	Date Purchased	Warranty Length	Expected Life	Purchase Price	Replacement Cost	Expected Replacement Date
Central air conditioner						
Clothes dryer						
Clothes washer						
Computer						
Dishwasher						
Furnace						
Garage door opener						
Lawn mower						
Microwave						
Printer						
Refrigerator						
Sofa						
Stereo						
Stove						
Sump pump						
Television						
Vacuum cleaner						
Water heater						

Now that you have an idea of how much money you need to keep in an account to be able to pay cash for these items as you need them, you can put these amounts in your budget. You may choose to save up the money for these items in your emergency fund, but we suggest that you set up a household expenses fund to cover them.

Taking Taxes into Account

You may have noticed that Table 2-2 does not deal with income taxes. Most people have their taxes deducted from their pay-cheques and don't need to deal with them separately until they file their tax returns.

As your investment plans bring in more dividends and income, or if you take on another job that doesn't deduct taxes (for example, a freelance or contract job), be sure to review your tax withholdings and adjust them as needed. Doing so prevents a big tax bill at the end of the year; you avoid penalties, too. If you have investments that are consistent under-performers, you might want to sell them by the end of the year to free up cash. You can use those losses to offset any investment gains, reducing your tax bill.

If, however, you're getting refunds — especially large refunds (you get to define large for yourself) — you need to make adjustments so that the taxes you pay throughout the year better reflect your liability. A refund is *not* "found money." It is money that you loaned to the government without earning interest on it.

Some reasons that you may be getting a refund:

- You haven't claimed the number of deductions to which you're entitled. Be sure to adjust your deductions as your family situation changes.
- You deliberately paid additional taxes because you expected to earn outside income from which tax deductions would not be taken; then you didn't earn that income.

- Your employer is deducting too much according to the number of dependants you're claiming, or you haven't updated your deductions as your circumstances have changed.
- You worked overtime. The tax table assumes that you were making that income every week, resulting in too much tax being withheld.

Paying Yourself First

Paying yourself first is one of the best money management decisions you can make. Simply put, paying yourself first means that you put money into a savings program to meet your short-term, mid-term, and long-term goals (see Chapter 1) *before* you pay anything else — including your rent or mortgage! If you're living from paycheque to paycheque, you may think that you can't do this. But determining where you spend your money shows you how you can pay yourself first and gain many benefits.

One thing you discovered when you tracked how you spent your money in the past is that emergencies always get paid somehow. If an insurance payment came due, you scrimped on restaurant meals or entertainment so that you had enough money to pay that important bill *before* your insurance was cancelled.

If you can "find" the money when you absolutely *must* have it, then you can live on less than you've been spending. The obvious conclusion is that you can put money aside for savings if you respect yourself enough to pay yourself first.

Chapter 5 goes into detail about lowering your expenses. For now, it's enough to identify the money that you didn't need to spend. Put that money in the savings category of your budget. When the insurance payment came due, for example, you told yourself that you didn't have money to spend on restaurant meals or movies. Isn't your future at least as important as paying for your insurance?

You'll find that when you have savings (and you *will*), the lowered stress, greater stability, feeling of financial security, and general well-being you enjoy are worth much more than the time and effort you invest in creating and maintaining your budget.

Setting Up a Basic Budget

Back in Table 2-2, you figured out where your money has been going. Discovering and dealing with your spending personality type gives you hints on how to change your habits to create a realistic budget and keep it up to date. This section shows you how to set up a budget that reflects the reality of your current financial life.

Remember that budgeting software, as discussed in Chapter 2, can help you create and maintain your budget.

Table 3-3 is a sample budget to show you what your budget might look like. Using the information from your spending diary, insert the values for what you paid in each category last month in the Last Month Actual column. After you determine what you should be spending in each category, put those amounts in the This Month Budget column. At the end of another month, put the amount that you actually spent in each category in the This Month Actual column.

This budget leaves you space in the Over/Under column to compare each item's real value with its real cost. When you compile your budget, you want to be able to compare real versus projected values on a monthly, quarterly, and yearly basis.

Note that these categories are not the same as those in Table 2-2. You'll determine which categories you need to include, so we want to show you how budget worksheets can vary. Choose categories that reflect your situation.

Table 3-3: My Monthly Budget

Expense	Last Month Actual	This Month Budget	This Month Actual	Over/Under
Housing and Utilities				
Mortgage* or rent	$	$	$	$
Homeowners'or condo assn. fees	$	$	$	$
Electricity	$	$	$	$
Gas	$	$	$	$
Water	$	$	$	$
Telephone (home and mobile)	$	$	$	$
Home maintenance	$	$	$	$
Subtotal, Housing and Utilities	$	$	$	$
Food				
Groceries	$	$	$	$
Restaurant meals	$	$	$	$
Subtotal, Food	$	$	$	$
Clothing and Shoes				
Adult 1	$	$	$	$
Adult 2	$	$	$	$
Child 1	$	$	$	$
Child 2	$	$	$	$
Subtotal, Clothing and Shoes	$	$	$	$
Child Care	$	$	$	$

Expense	Last Month Actual	This Month Budget	This Month Actual	Over/Under
Insurance				
Auto	$	$	$	$
Health	$	$	$	$
Homeowner's*/ renter's	$	$	$	$
Life	$	$	$	$
Other	$	$	$	$
Subtotal, Insurance	$	$	$	$
Health care				
Chiropractor	$	$	$	$
Doctor	$	$	$	$
Optometrist	$	$	$	$
Other practitioner	$	$	$	$
Eyeglasses, contact lenses	$	$	$	$
Prescriptions	$	$	$	$
Other	$	$	$	$
Subtotal, Health care	$	$	$	$
Auto				
Gasoline 1	$	$	$	$
Gasoline 2	$	$	$	$
Maintenance 1	$	$	$	$
Maintenance 2	$	$	$	$
Payment 1	$	$	$	$
Payment 2	$	$	$	$
Tolls	$	$	$	$
Taxis and public transportation	$	$	$	$
Subtotal, Auto	$	$	$	$

continued

Building a Budget

Expense	Last Month Actual	This Month Budget	This Month Actual	Over/Under
Personal				
Charitable contributions	$	$	$	$
Cosmetics	$	$	$	$
Entertainment	$	$	$	$
Haircuts	$	$	$	$
Magazines/ newspapers	$	$	$	$
Membership dues	$	$	$	$
Vacations	$	$	$	$
Other	$	$	$	$
Subtotal, Personal	$	$	$	$
Savings and Investments				
Savings/money market account	$	$	$	$
Education fund	$	$	$	$
Mutual fund	$	$	$	$
New car fund	$	$	$	$
New home fund	$	$	$	$
Retirement fund	$	$	$	$
Emergency savings account	$	$	$	$
Other	$	$	$	$
Subtotal, Savings and Investments	$	$	$	$

Expense	Last Month Actual	This Month Budget	This Month Actual	Over/Under
Taxes				
Federal income tax	$	$	$	$
Provincial income tax	$	$	$	$
CPP/EI	$	$	$	$
Property tax*	$	$	$	$
Subtotal, Taxes	$	$	$	$
TOTAL EXPENSES	$	$	$	$
Income				
Gross wages 1	$	$	$	$
Gross wages 2	$	$	$	$
Interest income	$	$	$	$
Alimony/ child support paid to you	$	$	$	$
Other	$	$	$	$
TOTAL INCOME	$	$	$	$
Difference between income and expenses (put shortages in parentheses)				
	$	$	$	$

* Often, your mortgage, property taxes, and insurance are lumped together in one payment. Don't "charge" yourself twice if you pay these expenses as part of your mortgage payments.

Make sure to account for all your expenses, but put them in any category that makes your budget work for you. For example, you may want to put your homeowner's or renter's insurance under Housing and Utilities rather than under Insurance. Moving items to other categories will reflect how you spend your money; your budget will reflect how you want to allocate your resources. Also, as you recognize new items, add them to your budget.

Remember that budgeting software can automatically prepare reports for you. Putting some of this information in graph form may make it easier for you to make comparisons and see changes.

Being Realistic

Remember that a budget is just a piece of paper.

How does a budget become and remain realistic? When the figures you enter in your budget reflect reality and not wishful thinking, when you're willing to spend time to update your budget regularly, and when you recognize that changes need to be made and make them.

Not being realistic has more consequences than a failed budget. Failure begets failure. If you allow yourself to stop planning realistically for your future, your stress level will rise and you'll waste time reacting to situations rather than acting on decisions you've made.

CHAPTER 4

sticking to your budget

IN THIS CHAPTER

- Understanding the role of self-discipline in financial planning
- Controlling your impulse spending
- Recognizing the people who can help you stay on course
- Dealing with emergency expenses
- Learning how to make using a budget a habit

Realizing that you need a budget, gathering your information, and putting that information into a usable form are giant strides toward securing your financial future. This chapter shows you how to build on the foundation that you established by creating a budget.

Good Discipline Equals Good Budgeting

You have many good habits that took time to cultivate. Sometimes it's hard to remember them; once you have a good habit, you don't really think about it until you start to lose it. Give yourself credit for developing habits such as these:

- I brush my teeth every day.
- I change the oil in my car regularly.
- I send birthday cards to my friends and family.
- I get to work on time.

In the interest of appreciating that you can learn budgeting habits, too, check off in the following list those good habits that you've already picked up

- ❑ I pay my bills on time.
- ❑ I balance my chequebook.
- ❑ I compare prices when I shop.
- ❑ I verify the charges on my credit card statement.

None of these habits, by themselves, will make your life either wonderful or awful. But adding good habits on top of good habits improves your life immensely.

You can't just fling your old bad habits out the window. To learn to be an effective budgeter, you must coax yourself into developing good habits. Check off the following activities that you can accomplish:

- ❑ Recognize how budgeting benefits me
- ❑ Notice changes in my spending habits and decide whether the changes are good or bad

☐ Revise my budget when my circumstances change
☐ Seek help when I need more information
☐ Set aside time every week to review my budget
☐ Write down changes that I want to make instead of keeping them in my head

Failing to use and revise your budget has many drawbacks:

• You waste the time that you already spent collecting data.
• You miss out on the many benefits that budgeting brings to your financial life, such as the ability to use decisions you've made rather than react to situations.
• Your stress level rises.
• You don't feel good about yourself.

Reining In Your Impulse Spending

If, every time you return from the store, you have more items than you intended to purchase, you're not entirely at fault. Store managers have studied consumers for years. Stores purposely use floor plans that tempt you to buy things you didn't know you wanted and expose you to as many buying opportunities as possible. For example, why is milk, probably the most-purchased item in any supermarket, at the back of the store? Those wily store managers know that if you have to look at long aisles of tempting items going to and from picking up your milk, your shopping cart will very likely have more than milk in it.

Don't confuse good buys with impulse purchases. If you buy something half-price that your family uses and you'll definitely finish it before it spoils, that's a good buying decision. Unless, that is, it means that you don't have the cash to pay another bill and will have to pay a penalty.

Recognizing your triggers

Previously, you may not have thought of your purchases as being "triggered." But if the milk scenario seems familiar to you, then you have your own triggers. Common triggers are

- **Fatigue:** You're worn out; you deserve a treat.
- **Hunger:** You don't have the energy to make a decision, so you treat yourself to junk food rather than a nutritious meal.
- **Overwork:** You've worked hard, so you feel that you deserve a reward.
- **Money in your pocket:** You have the cash to pay for it, so why not buy it?
- **Depression:** You try to make yourself feel better by treating yourself.
- **Elation:** You feel fantastic, so you buy yourself a little something to celebrate.
- **Occasion:** You or your friend/sister/brother/college roommate should surely have a nice present to mark a birthday/anniversary/new job.
- **Competition:** You have to give the nicest gift, or at least one that's as nice as so-and-so's.
- **The desire to impress someone:** You think, "Wait until so-and-so sees this!"

Assuring your long-term financial health is the best "treat" you can give yourself at any time!

You probably know the kinds of things you're most likely to purchase on a whim. Go to that area of your house and *write down* those things that you've purchased so that you can see how much money you've wasted by not making thoughtful decisions.

For example, are tools your weakness? Do you find it impossible to pass by a hardware store? Then take your survey in your workshop, garage, or tool shed. Or do you love buying yourself clothes? Then go to your closet. See the jacket you bought because the colour was beautiful? Of course, you have nothing that goes with it. How many items were on sale but don't really work well with the rest of your wardrobe?

Write down every item that falls into the impulse-spending category. You don't need to go through every closet or find every impulse purchase, but do write down all the impulse buys that you find in plain sight.

You'll use the list that you make in the next section. If you're part of a couple or you're doing this exercise with your children, everyone should be reassured before you start this survey that its only purpose is to gather information.

If you use your survey to find fault with your or others' purchases, you'll defeat the purpose and discourage helpful suggestions.

Before you go on, write an estimated cost next to each item. Then put a plus sign (+) next to anything you think you have used as much as you should have for the price. For example, you may have used your sailboat over several weekends every summer, but that means that it has still cost you $1,500 each time you used it for several hours — no + there. And don't forget the cost to insure that expensive toy.

Now put an asterisk (*) next to each item for which you could have found a reasonable substitute or alternative at a lower cost. We're not talking about something that arbitrarily went on sale, but something for which a small investment of time would have resulted in paying a much lower price. (In the case of the sailboat, for example, could you have found someone to share ownership, dividing the costs of both the boat and the insurance?) Next to the asterisk, write the price you think that you could have paid for a reasonable substitute or alternative.

Don't ignore small impulse purchases. Although you may not have included those items on this list, you purchase them more often, so they add up quickly.

Focusing on your goals

In Chapter 1, you made a list of your short-term, mid-term, and long-term goals. Retrieve that list now. You've gathered other information since then, so you'll probably want to revise the list before you work on eliminating impulse spending.

Now look at your revised goals list. Starting at the top of your list, apply the "overspent" amount from your impulse-buying list to paying for your goals, whether your goals are to pay off your debts, save more, start investing, or purchase something you really need or want. You may need to take more than one overspent amount to make up one goal amount. Don't bother to prioritize your goals here; you just want to know how many goals you could have checked off your goals list if you had not made impulse purchases. For example, not buying that sailboat would have covered many car payments.

Stopping yourself from making a purchase

Now that you recognize what makes you indulge in impulse spending and what the payoff can be when you make informed purchases based on your financial goals, you can control your triggers. You can do so by making conscious decisions *before* the temptation to buy reaches out to grab you.

Setting your "stop" triggers doesn't mean that you never get to treat yourself. If the supermarket is your downfall, for example, give yourself a set amount to spend any way you like. After a few trips to the store during which you can't decide what one treat you want, you'll find that you don't want any of them all that much!

If your impulse triggers go off in the hardware store or another type of store that sells big-ticket items, again give yourself a "treat budget." If you don't have enough money to buy what you want today, you can save up your treat allowance until you have enough money in that "account." But you don't get to buy now and pay with your future allowance!

Rounding Up Your Support Team

All kinds of people and organizations are around to help you meet your goals. In the case of people, you need to know why they want to help you, how much time and energy they can offer, and what their individual money personalities are. You may want to review the section on identifying money personalities at the end of Chapter 2 before you assign helping roles to your support team.

Spouse/significant other

The best way to work as a team with your spouse or significant other is to agree on your goals and which of them are most important. You may have to compromise on individual goals in order to reach your goals as a couple or family.

Often, one partner is a better money manager than the other. That partner may be better at resisting temptation, computing amounts, dividing long-term goals into mid-term and short-term goals, setting priorities, budget balancing, and so on. Or one partner may be better at some activities while the other handles the remaining tasks.

The secret to a good partnership is agreeing on goals and how you're going to reach those goals. Then each partner does the best job possible for his or her responsibilities. In spite of the word *partner*, you may decide to give one person more authority than the other — as long as you both agree on who should have more authority when it comes to financial matters, and you remember that financial security, not "being in charge," is your goal. As time goes on and changes need to be made, use the same negotiating and compromise that brought you as far as you are to help you set up a new system.

Children

If you have children, you certainly want to involve them in learning how to handle money. Keeping children involved in the budgeting process also helps them learn the financial lessons that they need to know at each stage in their lives.

For example, when Charles's children started getting allowances, he deducted 10 percent from each child's allowance. Needless to say, the first few deductions caused much upset. The lesson was that adults don't get to keep all they earn because they must pay taxes. Just as adults get police and fire protection and roads to drive on from their taxes, the children got a place to live, meals, and vacations from their "taxes."

When the children's dog got sick, they had to use part of their savings to help pay the veterinarian's bill. They learned what savings were for and how they could meet goals by saving today.

No child is too young to participate in the family budget. But the younger a child is, the shorter-term the goal must be to fit with young children's shortened attention span and patience. If your children are not part of your "budgeting board of directors," everyone gets cheated. They not only miss out on important lessons, but their feelings and wishes are not reflected in two strategic parts of family life: budgeting and buying decisions.

Parents

Your parents have lived longer and met and survived more financial challenges than you have. Their individual and collective money personalities are important as to what kinds of help they can provide and what kinds of help you want from them.

If your parents can handle requests for loans and advice in a businesslike manner (and if you'll respond with an equally businesslike attitude), you can ask for loans and advice. If they have the attitude that whoever pays gets to make the rules, they'll probably want more control and expect answers to more questions than you're willing to give them. If you're desperate for their help, one of the compromises you may have to live with is that you must live with their money personalities.

Just as you would negotiate the conditions of a new job before you accept it, you must negotiate the terms of your parents' involvement in your financial life before you agree to open that door.

Friends

Friends have many of the same pluses and minuses that parents do, except you aren't required to keep them forever. One of the benefits of friends' involvement in helping you reach your goals is that you can restrict them to just one area of your financial decision-making. You may think you know your friends well, but when money enters the picture, personalities can clash. If a friend gives you a loan, draw up a written agreement on the amount of the loan, when it is to be repaid, and how much interest is to be paid. If your friend suddenly decides that the loan gives them permission to tell you how to run your business or your life or your child's life, remind your "friend" of the contract.

Still, you may identify friends from whom you'd like advice on your finances. You can invite those friends into your financial circle based on your ability to work with the strengths and weaknesses of each person's money personality. If someone is a closer friend to one marriage partner than the other, the two of you must discuss and negotiate that factor as well. As you set financial priorities, your good relations with your partner must take precedence over getting advice or help from a friend.

Professional and free services

Professional sources can help you gather information, set goals, set priorities, or stay on your financial path. You can use these sources from the start, use them once in a while, or even discard them from your financial life once their purpose has been served.

Accountants do much more than fill out tax returns. They can help you set goals, remind you of factors that you have forgotten or ignored, use their backgrounds with a variety of people's problems and solutions to help you, start you on a good financial plan no matter what your age or income, help you revise your plans and goals as you get older, and — the part you'll probably enjoy the most — help you reduce the taxes you pay.

Depending on your accountant's practice, you may also be able to get information about estate planning, insurance practices, and housing.

Your employer, union, or trade organization may have an *EAP (Employee Assistance Program)*. The services that an EAP offers vary from provider to provider. Although some services may not be strictly financial, getting free or low-cost services in any area of concern will positively affect your financial situation and your ability to reach your goals.

Some EAPs offer budgeting, savings, tax, and estate planning services, either individually or in groups. The programs may also offer substance abuse help, family or individual counselling, workshops on buying and maintaining a home, and credit counselling. Whatever the topic, if you need information about it and don't pay for it, you've eliminated that budget expense while still learning what you need to know.

Your place of worship, community groups, credit bureaus, libraries, schools, financial institutions, and associations (such as alumni groups and Rotary clubs) may offer budgeting and savings programs, either free or at a low cost. Look in local newspapers and newsletters for ads announcing such programs. Your local library or social service agency may also keep track of such listings.

The program offerings from these groups may also include:

- Avoiding repair costs through regular maintenance
- Building (or rebuilding) a good credit rating
- Buying the right amount of insurance for you
- Evaluating banking services
- Handling credit wisely
- Avoiding the hidden costs of holiday shopping
- Learning about programs that help pay for education, health care, housing, and utilities
- Managing money
- Purchasing your first home
- Surviving a layoff or divorce

Many suppliers of such services offer customized programs.

Dealing with Emergency Expenses

Unexpected expenses can severely disrupt your financial status. The three situations that usually get people in financial trouble are:

- Accident or illness
- Expensive appliances that wear out
- Vehicle repair and replacement

Those expenses are the reason you have an emergency expense fund. (If you don't, go back to Chapter 3 and revise your budget!) If your fund isn't large enough, however, you can take short-term actions to avoid ending up in a spiral of debt:

- If your income is low, ask the local government and social services agency if low- or no-interest loans are available for these types of emergencies. Religious organizations also may have such funds.
- Ask your credit card companies and other creditors to let you skip a payment without penalty. They'll still add an interest charge, which raises your total debt, but the tactic frees up immediate money so that you can take care of the emergency.
- Pawn some possessions. Pawning is really a secured loan — you get cash in exchange for an item of value. If you pay back the loan (with interest, of course) by the deadline, you can retrieve your item.
- If you have a medical emergency, ask your health care provider about available services that would offset expenses for you, such as free or low-cost housing while your loved one is in the hospital and free or low-cost meals.

- If your problem is with your car and you have a good relationship with a garage, try to negotiate a time-payment plan at low or no interest (rather than the higher rate that you would be paying on your credit card).
- Take out a home-equity loan or second mortgage. Interest rates are usually much lower than what you'd pay on credit card debt, but read the fine print. On some of those loans, you could lose your house if you miss one loan payment. Make sure, too, that you have the right to pay the loan off early to cut the interest expense.
- If you belong to a social or service organization, find out whether it has a formal or informal system for helping members. For example, a student from Norway who came to study in Canada discovered that because of a miscommunication, he had arrived two weeks before his housing was available. He was a member of Mensa, so he called the local contact. Someone in the group put him up, rent-free, for the two weeks — and gave him a tour of the local area, topped off with a Labour Day picnic.

Be creative. This is another situation in which knowing the financial (and other) personality of your family members and friends helps. Either the boldest family member or friend, or the one with the strongest "saver" personality, will be the best negotiator for these perks.

Paying for an emergency by credit card may get you in debt at a high interest rate. If you *must* use a credit card, be sure to choose the one with the lowest interest rate. Now may be the time to take advantage of a low-introductory-rate card that has been offered to you — but do so *only* if you can pay off the balance before the end of the introductory rate expires, or if the regular rate is reasonable.

If at First You Don't Succeed . . .

Most psychologists say that cultivating a new habit takes 21 days. Doing something every day can change your life in three short weeks. Some financial habits are cultivated daily — packing lunches versus eating out, taking the bus versus taking a taxi, watching television versus going to a movie, listening to the radio versus downloading new music, and so on. Good habits in these categories can be acquired quickly. Other financial matters — like furniture and appliance shopping, choosing investment instruments, and so on — aren't things that you do every day, so learning new habits may take a little longer.

The Greek philosopher Aristotle said, "We are what we repeatedly do. Excellence is not an act, but a habit." You've already taken the time and trouble to gather information, study your partners in financial planning, learn new techniques, learn how to find help and new information, and set a budget and priorities. You wouldn't have pursued your goals with this amount of effort if you were going to give up at the first disappointment.

Humans make strange choices sometimes. Instead of giving ourselves credit for what we have accomplished, we only worry about what we still lack. Don't fall into this pit of disappointment! As you review your budget, take time to savour how far you've come, then pick which habit you want to tackle next and concentrate on it.

You don't want to wait an entire year to see whether your spending is on track with your budget. At a minimum, check quarterly — monthly is better.

CHAPTER 5

reducing expenses and increasing your income

IN THIS CHAPTER

- Analyzing how you currently spend your money
- Cutting your expenses
- Learning to make efficient financial choices
- Determining whether you need to make more money

Reducing your expenses may sound like a negative experience. Think of all the things you'll have to do without! When you finish this chapter, however, you'll feel the delight of having your spending under control. A bonus is the disappearance of stress from not knowing how you're going to pay your bills and plan for your future. Because you'll have made spending decisions before you even leave your home, and because you'll know that sticking to those decisions will help you meet your goals, you won't spend time and energy on every spending decision.

If your best planning still finds "more month than money," the solution is to increase your income. Like you never thought of that, right? The difference is that in the past, your "plan" consisted of dreaming "if only I made more money." Here, you'll learn how to figure the amount you need, how to determine whether your need is short-term or long-term, and exactly where you can find your personal pot of gold.

Finding Alternatives to Spending

In Chapter 1, you gathered your bank and credit card statements. Then you used various coloured highlighters to categorize your purchases. Look over those records again and update your categories. (If you're using computer software to track your finances, you can use it to categorize your spending as well.)

As you categorize your spending, you can change your categories or even add and subtract categories. One important note to remember is that your system shouldn't frustrate you to the point that you stop your efforts to control your spending. Your financial health is important, so make it easy.

Spend, rent, borrow, or co-own?

When the lawn is as high as an elephant's eye, do you go out and buy a lawn mower? Doing so would seem logical ... except that your lawn takes only half an hour to mow. Once a week. Maximum.

Does your neighbour have the hugest, most magnificent maple tree in the province — with piles of autumn leaves in the yard to go with it? Raking all those leaves is a big job — for one month out of 12.

Earlier in this book, you started a list of everything you own. Expand that list by adding things that you forgot and then writing down what each item cost and how often you use it. Until you decided to get control of your spending, you probably thought that you needed each of these things because you actually use them. Listing how much they cost and how often you use them gives you a whole new perspective.

Remember that the cost of insuring, maintaining, and storing rarely used items is an ongoing expense, even on appliances that are paid for. Make sure to factor these costs into your list.

For each item that you own but rarely use, you have five choices:

- Keep it and use it until it wears out
- Sell shares in the appliance to friends and neighbours who also have only intermittent need of the item
- Sell the item and then rent or borrow a replacement only when you have a need for it
- Sell the item and then pay someone to perform that chore with his or her own equipment
- Find a lower-cost alternative to the item

After you pick one of these five choices, put a new cost on each item in your list. How much money could you free up by renting, borrowing, or co-owning?

Now that you have this information, how will you use it? The four choices tell you not only what to do with your current appliances, but also how to handle future needs. For example, when the leaf blower can't huff and puff anymore, you have five choices:

- Replace it
- Rent a leaf blower only when the leaves come tumbling down

- Find friends and neighbours who have the same need, pool your money to purchase a new leaf blower, and take turns using it
- Make arrangements to borrow someone else's leaf blower when the need arises
- Use a rake

Whether you're renting, borrowing, or co-owning, make sure that your "partners" share your attitude on maintenance, cleanup, storage, and general care of tools and appliances.

Spend or barter?

With the proper incentive, anyone can make a deal. You may say that you don't know how to barter, but return for a minute to your childhood, and you'll see that you've always had the skill. Remember the words, "But Mom, if you buy me this toy, I'll eat all my vegetables for a week"?

Even in the grown-up world, you have negotiating skills — and bartering is negotiating. Maybe you want your washing machine fixed, your lawn mowed, or your eavestroughs cleaned out. All you need to do is find something that you can do for someone else in return for the service you need. For example, you help a friend with his resumé and, in exchange, he helps build you some bookshelves.

You have skills to trade, too. Think about the things you can do that other people want done for them. Make a list of all the skills you use at work or in pursuing your hobbies — filling out tax returns, hanging wallpaper, taking photographs, and so on. Remember that personal skills (for example, closet reorganizing) and thinking skills (for example, planning a vacation) are tradable, too.

Using a fresh piece of paper (or a new computer file), start a list of all your skills. Keep this list with you. As you go about your life, you'll think of more and more skills to add to this list. You may want to divide the list into things you're willing to do, things you'll do if you have to, and things you don't ever want to do again.

Consider bartering clubs, which may facilitate this part of your money management. To find a bartering club, look in your local Yellow Pages, search the Internet (type "barter club" and the name of your city), ask a librarian, or check with neighbourhood organizations, professional and trade associations, service organizations, alumni associations, and churches.

Every club has its own rules, but, like any other organization, someone has to pay the organization's costs. These include accounting, mail costs, promotion fees, and so on. If you're interested in joining a bartering club, you need to know the following information:

- Is there a fee to join? An annual fee?
- What fees are assessed on barters?
- Who belongs now? (Get a list.)
- Are the club membership and services growing or shrinking?
- How long has the club been in existence?
- Can you drop your membership whenever you want, as long as you "pay" whatever outstanding "debt" is in your account?

Find out as much as you can about a club before you join. If other members aren't reliable, are so fussy that they'll always complain about your contribution, or live so far away that they can't fulfill your needs, don't join. Keep in mind as well that Canada

Revenue Agency recognizes and accounts for one barter dollar as equivalent to one Canadian dollar, so you have to report earnings and expenses of barter dollars just as you would cash.

Making Over Your Lifestyle

Giving your lifestyle a makeover is not the same as lowering your standard of living or depriving yourself. In fact, it can be quite the opposite. The emphasis here is on *style*. As the preceding sections on sharing and bartering demonstrate, a lifestyle makeover involves an attitude shift that will help you get the most for your dollar. The following sections will help you reach your financial goals.

Use coupons rather than pay full price

The art of saving money by using coupons has become a consumer industry in itself. Whether you've never used coupons or you use them and want to get more from your efforts, the tips in this section can help you meet your goals.

"Couponing" is a skill for which reading carefully really pays off. First, you have to find coupons. Check newspapers and newspaper inserts, the packaging of items you've already bought, the back of your supermarket receipts, and coupon trade boxes inside stores, to name a few sources. Or try online sources such as smartcanucks.ca and save.ca.

You can get more than face value for your coupons by shopping at stores that "double," or give you twice what the coupon is worth.

Don't buy something just because you have a coupon for it. If you won't use the product for a while, you have to store it; if it's something you don't like, you'll never use it. As well, even with a coupon, prepared foods are often more expensive — not to mention less healthy — than home-made meals.

Keep up with the Joneses, but get better deals

Warehouse clubs like Costco can come to your aid with special deals. Because these organizations buy in bulk, they often get a lower rate and can pass those savings along to you.

If you're planning a car trip and a gasoline credit card offers hotel discounts, this may be the time to obtain that card. If you have trouble with overspending on credit cards, you can close out your account as soon as the trip is over.

Remember that you don't have to spend a lot to have fun

When you first determined to get your financial house in order, you probably thought that entertainment was going to go by the wayside. Even with cable, television is a pretty poor long-term amusement. Luckily, you have many other options.

If the theatre, the opera, live music, and so on are your passion, you can enjoy them without breaking your budget. Many of these events use volunteer ushers. You usher; you attend for free. The downside is that you may have to see the same play 10 times — and you can't walk out on a stinker. In the long run, however, you'll have a good time without spending a lot of money.

Some travel agencies sell off cruises and other deals at very good prices to people who can fill vacancies at the last minute. You can buy into these deals at 50 percent or less of the listed price. Sometimes you have to become a member of a travel group's club in order to be notified of an opening. Will you use or save enough to make membership fees worthwhile? These discounted offers are great, especially for retirees and self-employed people, whose schedules are flexible.

Spend less and enjoy life more

Look for your own opportunities to reduce your expenses without reducing your quality of life. Instead of always looking to your wallet to pay for entertainment, use the creative skills that you've been developing. Knowledgeable, reliable people are in demand everywhere.

- Does your child's class need a chaperone for a school trip? Volunteer for the job.
- If you can't devote the time to be a regular usher at a theatre, offer a skill or time in trade for attending a dress rehearsal.
- If you like sports, find out what personnel are needed to put on an event. Could you be an assistant coach for a children's soccer or baseball league? Can you help organize a local tennis tournament?
- Can you speak a second language? Offer a friend language lessons in exchange for her teaching you to play guitar.
- Need a babysitter? Why not trade nights with other parents? You can take all the kids for a sleepover with the understanding that the parents will reciprocate, giving you a whole night off. What bliss!

Living on less

If you went to the store to buy one size and brand of bread and could pay either $2.50 or $3.00 for it, which would you choose? Sounds like a dumb question, doesn't it? Yet every day, people make the wrong decision.

Here are some ways to live on less without sacrificing quality of life:

- Shop at discount stores instead of convenience stores, and buy the same items for less. Head to the library or browse the Internet for a local or area-wide directory of discount and outlet stores.
- Take your lunch to work instead of buying it; you'll have a healthier lunch and save money, too.
- Negotiate with your employer to work at home. You can save restaurant, travel, car wear-and-tear, and clothing expenses.

  Negotiate who is going to pay for the equipment, telephone lines, and other expenses. If those expenses are your responsibility, you may be spending instead of saving money.
- Understand your real goal before you make a purchase. If you want to lose weight, you can do so for free by walking in the park or by taking advantage of the company gym. Either one is cheaper than signing a contract at an exercise facility.
- A used car is "new" to you. Not only do you pay less, but your insurance costs are less than on a new car, your depreciation is slower, and you don't have to dread that first ding in the door.
- Always use a shopping list. Just as the lines on the highway keep you driving in the lane, a shopping list keeps you from giving in to temptation. Even if you decide to purchase something not on your list, you will have considered and weighed the purchase.

Hanging On to Your "Found" Money

The fastest way to undo all your hard work is to think of your money as a tradeoff between spending on one item and spending on another. Yes, you can take advantage of the savings that come from buying in quantity — if you've allowed for waste, storage costs, and the other possible expenses of having a large quantity of one item on hand.

If you release yourself from always worrying about money by reducing your expenses, you may feel "rich" because you have cash in your pocket at last. That "found" money should go first toward debt reduction (as Chapter 6 discusses in depth) and then to savings (see Chapter 7).

Does paying off debts and then putting money toward savings mean that you don't get to enjoy the fruits of your labour? Of course not. You get to enjoy being free from worry, seeing your debts disappear, and watching your savings grow.

While you're paying off debts and starting a savings program with your "found" money, don't even think about the credit available on your credit cards. Using that credit means more debt, which is exactly what you don't want.

Earning Additional Income

If all your money-saving, coupon-clipping, and planning still leaves you short of achieving your goals, look for ways to earn more income. Getting a raise would be nice — and it's even possible! To find out what others doing your job are earning, contact trade associations, your alumni association, and unions, and do research at the library or on the Internet (try payscale.com for a free salary report based on your job title, location, and education).

If your wage is lower than average, take your research to your boss and ask for a raise.

Also, in the same way that you took inventory of your spending and your belongings, take an inventory of your skills. Look for skills that you use at work, but maybe aren't appreciated by your boss and aren't being recognized in your paycheque. Bosses don't have to think about what's going right ... so they don't! You need to remind your boss about your accomplishments. If you can prove that you're underpaid, negotiate a raise.

Do you have hobbies that can earn you extra money? For example, if you know how to work with wood, you can sell the furniture that you build or help people build things for a fee. You may have to do a little research to see how much you should charge customers, but hobbies still are a good source of income that's a pleasure to earn.

You not only need to survey your knowledge and skills to see where you might earn extra income, but you also must decide how much you want to earn and what it will cost you to do so. Remember to calculate material and tool expenditures as well as time expenditures. Will you recoup your investment? Will you have enough income to write off those expenditures on your income taxes as business expenses?

Think about whether you want to take on the extra work for a short, medium, or long period of time.

- **Short-term need:** If you want to do extra work only long enough to pay off your credit card or other debt, you may want to look for seasonal work or register with a temporary-employment agency. Because you won't be working extra for

a long time (you get to define "long"), you'll probably have
the energy to work longer hours, work more days per week,
commute a little farther, and so on.

- **Mid-term need:** If this extra job is going to go on for a
  while because you need the extra income for a longer period,
  such as while your child grows up, you don't want to commit yourself to so many hours, so much travel, or so many
  days per week that you don't have a life. That's a quick way
  to burn out. Not only will you fail to reach your goals, you'll
  be discouraged and may even think that you can't reach your
  goals or that budgeting doesn't work.

- **Long-term need:** Perhaps you've been a victim of the re-
  cession and you've lost a good job and had to take two lower
  paying jobs to make ends meet. Or maybe you've watched
  the value of your investments plunge and you've taken on
  a second job in order to earn extra income for a long-term
  need, such as retirement. Consider the same things that
  you did for a mid-term need. Recognize that the decisions
  you make will affect your lifestyle for a long time and guard
  against burnout.

If you're going to be forced to spend more time at work,
have more commuting costs, have wasted "dead" time (blocks of
time between jobs that are long enough to be annoying but short
enough that you can't really use them for naps, grocery shopping,
or whatever), it may be time to consider cutting back on your lifestyle. Moving to less-expensive housing, sharing housing, seeking
sales, bartering more aggressively, and so on, will allow you to
make more life-enhancing decisions sooner.

For mid-term or long-term extra income needs, consider
trading some of the income for cutting back on your lifestyle. The

tips in this chapter can help you make your money go further so that you can enjoy your life and still get out of debt and start a savings program.

CHAPTER 6

tackling your debt

IN THIS CHAPTER

- Totalling your debt
- Reviewing your spending plan to avoid adding to your debt
- Repaying your debts
- Deciding whether you need to consolidate your debts

By now (that is, if you've read Chapters 1 through 5), you must be convinced that a systematic plan is the secret to getting a handle on your finances. Although the choices you'll make about handling your debt may be somewhat complicated, you have all the skills and knowledge that you need to create an effective debt-repayment plan. This chapter shows you how to apply them.

Figuring Out How Much You Owe

To find out how much you owe, the first step is to do a personal debt survey. This survey is a little easier because you need only your latest statement from each debt. Gather the following documents:

- Mortgage payment schedule
- Automobile payment record
- Credit card statements
- Loan statements
- Paperwork for private loans from relatives and friends. (Keep good records so that no dispute occurs.)

On a piece of paper, or using your budgeting software or a spreadsheet program, create a table like Table 6-1. The information you gathered in Chapter 2 by surveying your chequebook records will help you do so quickly and completely.

To see how much your debt is costing you, call each lender and ask how much you paid in interest last year. Record those amounts in Table 6-1. Remember that you received *no* benefit from all that money you paid in interest.

Table 6-1: My Consumer Debt Register

Account	Total Amount Due	Monthly Payment	Total Interest Paid Last Year	Interest Rate
Visa	$4,568	$115	$639	12.9%
MasterCard	$2,372	$86	$481	15.9%
Home Repairs, Inc.	$1,423	$67	$314	18.5%
Car payment	$15,268	$236	$1,162	7.1%
Mortgage	$117,469	$916	$8,437	6.7%

Reducing Your Consumer Debt

Most financial planners warn that if your consumer debt is more than 20 percent of your monthly net income, you're probably going to have trouble keeping your head above water, financially speaking. In Table 6-1, is the total of your monthly payments below 20 percent of your net income? Don't feel good just yet. Your long-term goal is to pay off all your consumer debt every month so that you don't pay interest to anyone.

Make sure you know the details of your bank loans; sometimes there's a fee if you pay them off early. Credit unions are owned by their members, so they don't tend to have such hidden costs.

Pay off high-interest-rate credit cards first

Getting the balance on one of your credit cards down to $0 feels good. Because it seems to be a giant step toward the goal of having no consumer debt, many debtors pay extra money on their lowest-balance cards. That is *not* the way to speed up the reduction of your debt, however. Even if you make no new purchases, you end up paying interest on the interest you already were charged! How does that happen? Because your original debt *plus* the interest amount becomes the new amount on which next month's interest cost is based.

By paying off your high-interest-rate cards first, you save the most money. Tables 6-2 and 6-3 offer a comparison of how the interest rate affects your ability to pay off your debt. In this example, we used *simple interest* (computed monthly as a flat rate). Credit card companies and other credit debt holders often compute interest daily — in which case the effects of paying interest on interest are even more devastating!

Table 6-2: Your Debt Cost at 11.9 Percent Annual Interest

Month	Balance	Yearly Interest Rate ÷ 12	Interest Debt This Month	New Balance	Payment
1	$5,000.00	0.9916666%	$49.58	$5,049.58	$150.00
2	$4,899.58	0.9916666%	$48.58	$4,948.16	$150.00
3	$4,798.16	0.9916666%	$47.58	$4,845.74	$150.00
4	$4,695.74	0.9916666%	$46.57	$4,742.31	$150.00
5	$4,592.31	0.9916666%	$45.54	$4,637.85	$150.00
6	$4,487.85	0.9916666%	$44.50	$4,532.35	$150.00

Total interest paid in six months: $282.35
Total of payments for six months: $467.65
Percent of payoff that's interest: 50

Table 6-3: Your Debt Cost at 8.9 Percent

Month	Balance	Yearly Interest Rate ÷ 12	Interest Debt This Month	New Balance	Payment
1	$5,000.00	0.7416666%	$37.08	$5,037.08	$150.00
2	$4,887.08	0.7416666%	$36.25	$4,923.33	$150.00
3	$4,773.33	0.7416666%	$35.40	$4,808.73	$150.00
4	$4,658.73	0.7416666%	$34.55	$4,693.28	$150.00
5	$4,543.28	0.7416666%	$33.70	$4,576.98	$150.00
6	$4,426.98	0.7416666%	$32.83	$4,459.81	$150.00

Total interest paid in six months: $209.81
Total of payments for six months: $690.19
Percent of payoff that's interest: 30

Table 6-3 shows you that in just six months, you save $72.54 by paying a 3 percent lower annual interest rate. Your balance due at the lower rate is $222.54 less than at the higher rate. From this example, you can see how paying off your higher-rate cards first saves you money, gets you out of debt faster, and helps you pay less interest.

While there is no federal credit counselling agency, there are numerous provincial and regional ones. Take advantage of these non-profit groups, which provide their services free of charge. Credit Counselling Canada (creditcounsellingcanada.ca) offers an extensive listing by province. Some examples:

Credit Counselling Society of British Columbia, *nomoredebts.org.* 888-527-8999

Credit Counselling Services of Alberta, *moneyproblems.ca.* 888-294-0076 or 403-265-2201 or 780-423-5265

Credit Counselling Society of Saskatchewan, *nomoredebts.org.* 888-527-8999

Manitoba Community Financial Counselling Services, *cfcs.mb.ca.* 204-989-1900

Ontario Association of Credit Counselling Services, *indebt.org.* 888-746-3328

Unions du Consommateur, Montreal (French language only), 514-521-6820 or 888-521-6820

Credit Counselling Services of Atlantic Canada, *solveyourdebts.com.* 888-753-2227

Do not use credit repair services that you see advertised on telephone poles and construction-site hoardings. They can't do anything that you can't either do yourself, or use a free credit counselling service to do for you. On top of that, these fly-by-night firms charge for their "service" — money that you could have used to pay down your debt.

Use department store credit cards wisely — or not at all

As with other credit cards, there's a good way and a bad way to use department store credit cards. These cards tend to have high interest rates. That doesn't mean that you shouldn't use them at all; just use them wisely. Also, be aware that holding such cards means that you will be bombarded by mailings from those stores. You can learn about sales this way, but you may be tempted to buy things that you don't need.

As Chapter 5 advises, always shop with a list. Because you'll have taken an inventory of everything in your home and will keep that list up to date, you'll know whether you really need that beautiful new coat on the cover of the latest store mailer.

If you're trying to rebuild your credit, department store cards can be a good way to do so. They are relatively easy to get — if your credit rating isn't good, you just get a low maximum. And these cards don't charge annual fees. The combination gives you a chance to charge carefully, pay religiously, and improve your credit rating.

Department store card balances can sneak up on you. Along with high interest rates, these cards often have a low minimum payment due. As you learned earlier in this chapter, the longer you stretch out paying off the balance, the more interest you pay. And as Tables 6-2 and 6-3 demonstrate, higher interest rates make a big difference in a short time in the amount you have to pay back.

Stop using your credit cards

All habits can be a challenge to break. The real problem with breaking spending habits is that it's more like controlling food than controlling tobacco. As hard as it may be, you can avoid tobacco. But you have to eat, and you have to spend money. So the real secret is control, not abstinence.

Keep your goals in mind. Use your written budget, financial plan, and spending diary to keep yourself on track. Once you enjoy the lack of stress from overspending, can see yourself working toward your goals, and get to enjoy reaching personal as well as financial objectives, you'll make different choices.

One good thing about using credit cards is the statements. They give you, in an easily accessible form, information about your spending habits. If you can resist overspending and unplanned spending, you can use your credit cards again. Because your new way of handling credit cards will look good on your credit report, you'll be able to get lower-interest cards, lower-rate loans, and a lower-rate mortgage. Your good financial reputation will give you leverage to negotiate other financial deals.

Paying Back Your Loans

You handle loans like you handle consumer debt: You decide which loans to pay first, based on their rates. (The exception is mortgages, which you can read about later in this chapter.) And you want to avoid new debt.

As you do for consumer debt, if you run into a rough patch financially, call your lenders and make deals for deferring payments *before* your payments are late. But be very careful when you negotiate. The interest rate on some loans rises automatically if you're late or you defer payment(s). Negotiate to keep your interest rate the same!

When you've tallied six months or more of faithful payments, ask your creditors to lower your interest rates.

Student and educational loans

If you're sorry now that you took out those student loans, you still have a lot to learn about personal finance. Student loans are an investment in your future. Graduating from college or university is still a good investment, even after you pay off your loans. So take a deep breath, roll up your sleeves, and put the loan payback into your budget.

There are federal and provincial student loans and grants available for students in need. When you graduate from college or university, you have a six-month *grace period* on the loans — meaning you don't have to start making loan repayments for a full six months. (However, if you don't return to full-time studies, you are responsible for paying the interest accrued during this period.)

When the grace period ends, you must start paying back your loan. Although the principal amount of your monthly payment will be determined by the bank and is non-negotiable, you can choose between two payment options: the floating rate option (the prime lending rate plus 2.5 percent) or a fixed rate of prime plus 5 percent.

If you choose the floating rate, the interest rate charged to you changes whenever your bank announces a change in the prime rate. This could affect the time it takes to pay back your loan. By maintaining the same monthly payment amount, you will repay the loan in a shorter time if the interest rate declines. But, if the interest rate rises, you will be repaying the loan over a longer period of time to cover the additional interest charged to you on the principal. If you choose the fixed rate, the interest rate charged to you does not change during the term of your loan. The loan will be paid out by the end of your term, provided all payments are made on time.

Which plan is for you? Well, if you think interest rates will go up, go with a fixed rate plan; if you think they're going down, choose the floating rate. If in doubt, ask the advice of an investment professional.

You can negotiate your interest rate if you have a qualified guarantor. The guarantor signs an agreement with the bank stating he or she will repay your loan if you default on payment.

If you're having difficulty with your loan payments, there are two options:

- **Revision of terms:** You may be able to revise the terms of your loan if you are unable to meet your obligations due to being unemployed or underemployed. Contact your bank for more information.
- **Interest Relief:** The federal government and the governments of Newfoundland, Nova Scotia, Manitoba, New Brunswick, Ontario, and Alberta offer an interest relief program. You can apply to these governments for interest relief, and if you qualify, the government will pay the interest on your behalf.

If you still can't make your payments, your loan will go to the bank's collection department. Make every effort to ensure this doesn't happen — it could affect your credit rating, making it difficult for you to get things like a car loan or a mortgage in the future.

Certain governments have additional programs that will relieve some of your student loan debt. The government will determine if you qualify and then advise your bank directly of any changes to your loan. Contact your provincial government for more information.

Don't forget: When tax time comes, you can write off the interest paid on your student loan each year.

For a wealth of information on student loans, go to the National Student Loans Service Centre (NSLSC) website (https:// nslsc.canlearn.ca). In addition to allowing you to apply for and manage your student loans online, it offers neat functions like a repayment calculator, which shows how much your monthly payments would be at different interest rates. The Human Resources Development Canada site, rhdcc-hrsdc.gc.ca, is another excellent resource, offering a good explanation of how the student loan program operates, as well as eligibility requirements for loans and repayment assistance. For additional questions regarding student loans, call the Canadian Alliance of Student Associations, at 613-236-3457 or casa.ca.

Car loans

You want to pay off a car loan in the shortest time possible. The longer the term of the loan, the more you pay over the life of the loan. When you secure the loan, make sure that there is no prepayment penalty. Watch your dealership or lender contract carefully to avoid additional fees and penalties.

Mortgages

Your housing costs are part of your short-term, mid-term, and long-term goals, as shown in Chapter 1. But a budget is a living, changing thing. To meet your current goals, you may want to update your strategies.

If loan rates have fallen since you financed your home, now may be the time to renegotiate or refinance. Remember that there are costs associated with this process, such as application fees, points, and so on. (Points are a one-time only refinancing fee — one point is equal to 1 percent of your mortgage's value.) Will you be in the home long enough to recoup that money and save from the lower interest rate? If not, refinancing isn't for you.

If you do refinance, you need to be careful about the "small" things that can add big costs, just like you did when you first got a loan. Fees, penalties, closing costs, prepayment penalties, and so forth can wipe out your "savings" from refinancing very quickly. If you take a longer-term loan than you need, the interest rate may be lower than that on your current loan, but higher than the rate you would get on a shorter-term loan now. Try to refinance for the time it would take to pay off your current mortgage. Or use the lower interest to pay your current amount, but for a shorter time.

If you choose to pay more than you owe in any month, write a separate cheque and clearly mark it "for principal only." If you don't specify, the bank will pay itself first — that is, it will apply the money to interest instead of principal.

In general, your mortgage is the last debt you want to prepay. It probably has a lower interest rate than any other debt on your plate.

Consolidating Your Bills as a Last Resort

If you fill in Table 6-1, you can see how much you must pay every month just to pay the minimums on your credit card and loan debts. Add your mortgage or rent payment and monthly living expenses, and the total can be overwhelming.

If you can't meet your monthly obligations, no matter how well you budget or how much you can expect to earn from your job(s), you may need a consolidation loan. For this type of loan, the lender pays off all the obligations that you decide to put under the plan. That total is the amount of your loan. You then pay one manageable bill to the lender every month.

Sounds great, doesn't it? The problem is that the interest rate on the consolidation loan is probably as high as that on your *highest* previous debt, and the term is probably longer than that on your *longest* previous debt. Therefore, the cost to you over the term of the loan is much higher than the cost of paying off your debts under their original terms.

If your consolidation loan is secured by your home — a home equity loan — you can lose your home if you can't make your payments. Companies specialize in making these types of loans so that they can take possession of the property at the first missed payment. Unlike mortgage lenders that try to help borrowers keep their homes, the purpose of "shark" lenders is to profit by taking over property for as little investment as possible.

A consolidation loan looks bad on your credit record. The result may be that in the future, you'll have to borrow at a higher interest rate than if you had paid the debts without consolidating. But a consolidation loan looks a lot better than a default or bankruptcy!

CHAPTER 7

putting money away for the future

IN THIS CHAPTER

- Identifying your attitude toward risk
- Looking at the available savings and investing instruments
- Making decisions based on the length of time to your goal
- Tracking the performance of your investments

While creating a budget, you learned the multiple benefits of paying off your debts. Paying off debts not only erases the debts themselves, but also lets you stop wasting your money on interest and releases funds for investing. You want to make the most of those "found" dollars and invest them wisely.

This chapter shows you how to determine which types of savings and investment vehicles will work for you and your goals, and also shows you how to keep track of the investments in which you decide to put your money.

Identifying Your Saving and Investing Personality

You have a money personality (discussed in Chapter 2); you also have a personality that affects your savings and investment goals. Your saving and investing personality reflects how much risk you're willing to take for higher returns.

Risk tolerance is similar to an exerciser's pain tolerance. If you don't believe in pain, you have a low risk tolerance — you're willing to accept low interest rates in return for not worrying about your investments. If you think that you probably need to have a muscle twinge or two to see results, you have a moderate risk tolerance — you're willing to take some risk in pursuit of a higher return on investment. If you think that if you don't need medical care after your workout, you haven't really worked out, you have high tolerance of risk — you're willing to take big risks in hopes that your investments will grow fast and furiously, and you also feel that you can rebuild your financial foundation if you lose a bundle.

Identify your savings/investment personality from the following list:

- **Low risk-taker:** Your primary concern is to protect the money (principal) you have now. People who can't afford to have their nest eggs shrink at all — such as retirees, widows and widowers, and novice and low-income savers — fall into this group.

  Low risk-takers depend on compounding interest for growth in their savings plans. Savings accounts, GICs, and other "sure" investments are in their portfolios. These folks can't (or think that they can't) take risks. Retirees no longer have paycheques coming in to make up losses. Novice investors can't afford to lose the modest nest eggs they have because they'll fall far behind in their investment plans if they have to build those nest eggs again.

Worrying about the safety of your investments will not keep you up nights if you're a low risk-taker. During periods of economic growth, with stable prices but low interest rates, however, investors in this category can lose ground. Even the most committed low risk-takers must switch some funds to higher-yielding instruments so that inflation doesn't erode their buying power.

- **Moderate risk-taker:** A moderate risk-taker is more daring than a low risk-taker but is still a conservative investor. Moderates are often in the midst of their income-earning years. Their goals include putting their children through college or university and planning for retirement. Keeping even with inflation will not enable them to reach these goals. On the other hand, moderates don't want to go for the "big kill" (really high returns) because that strategy is accompanied by high risk.

  Moderates can take some risk because they're still in their income-earning years and, by changing their budgets, they can make up some of the loss from an investment gone bad.

- **High risk-taker:** High risk-takers look for large returns on their investments. Sometimes people who are just starting their careers are high risk-takers because they don't have family responsibilities; and, because they expect their incomes to increase, they have time to rebuild from a loss.

  Other high-risk investors are speculators who enjoy the thrill of hunting down that big return. Sometimes speculators take the time to be extremely well informed about investments and feel sure of them. Other times they're just lucky — or not.

Most people have parts of each personality. You may be a higher risk-taker when you know more about an investment, a low risk-taker when you're uninformed or thinking about protecting your core investment, and a moderate risk-taker when you know a little and feel somewhat confident.

Just as you have some of each investment personality in you, your investment *portfolio* (the group of investments that you hold) needs to reflect some of each type of risk. This setup makes the most of your investment dollars and enables you to reach your goals in a manner that's comfortable for you.

This type of investment mixture is called a *balanced portfolio*. Here, *balanced* doesn't mean investing the same amount in each risk category. Rather, you determine the amount to put in each risk category by taking into account your comfort level and your needs so that your portfolio works for you.

No one mixture of investments is best for everyone. For example, a low risk-taker needs to conserve capital. The goal is to assure having a nest egg, but to get some higher returns to at least balance the erosion of inflation. This person will probably want at least 50 percent of his or her portfolio to be in low-risk investment, perhaps 30 percent in moderate-risk, and 20 percent in high-risk. This mix provides a "safe base."

Someone who is even more fearful of losing his or her nest egg may invest even more conservatively. Low-risk investments may be 60 percent or more of this portfolio, with about 30 percent in moderate-risk and perhaps 10 percent in high-risk categories.

Even low risk-takers can be daring within their own parameters, though. A "daredevil" might divide the portfolio with 40 percent in low-risk investments, 30 percent in moderate-risk, and 30 percent in high-risk areas.

Understanding Different Savings and Investment Instruments

There's no one right savings or investment instrument for everyone, because the needs that shape your choices are unique. The following sections take a look at the most common instruments. (By the way, "savings and investment instruments" is just a fancy way of saying "where you keep your money.")

Savings accounts and money market accounts

Savings accounts and money market accounts are good places to save for short-term goals, such as buying a new piece of furniture. Because withdrawing your funds from one of these accounts is easy, you can take advantage of special deals as they come up.

The main difference between a savings account and a money market account is that a savings account is offered by a bank, and a money market account is offered by a mutual fund company. If you want to put money in either type of account, look for the highest interest rate, but make sure that no offsetting fees — like commissions, service fees, or penalties for withdrawal — apply, or that the cost of doing business with that institution doesn't eat up your interest (or even worse, your principal).

Banks may charge you a fee to keep a savings account with a low balance. If you keep a small sum in an account but the bank imposes a monthly, quarterly, or annual charge when your balance falls below a certain amount, then you may be better off keeping your money under your mattress.

Credit unions are a great way to avoid these types of fees. Credit unions are owned by their members, so they tend to have fewer service charges. You'll save on fees, and the interest rates on credit union loans and savings accounts are comparable to the rates that banks pay. Online banks often don't charge fees and pay higher interest rates than conventional banks. The only problem: you must have a conventional bank account before you can set up an account with an online bank.

GICs

GICs usually earn higher rates of interest than savings accounts do, but they don't have fees attached like mutual funds or stock or bond investments (described later in this section). Unlike a savings account, you can't add to the deposit or withdraw money before the GIC's maturity date without paying a penalty.

The good news with a GIC is that you know exactly what to expect. When you purchase a GIC, you agree to a certain return, unlike the fluctuating rate of a savings account. Obviously, you want to shop around for the highest rate.

Your GIC is due at a stated period, which may be months or years. (The longer the term, the higher the rate of return.) When that date comes, you may reinvest or take your earnings. If you cash in your GIC before its due date, you have to pay a penalty.

If you have a GIC or similar account that charges a penalty for taking out cash before a certain date and you use this account to pay bills, you are, in effect, throwing money away. You lose the amount of the penalty and get nothing to show for it. It's like going out to dinner and paying for your meal, but not being allowed to eat it. If you need cash while you have money tied up in a GIC, you may be better off taking out a loan by using the GIC for security. You avoid the early-withdrawal penalty, which may be more than the cost of the loan.

RRSPs

Registered Retirement Savings Plans (RRSPs) are voluntary retirement savings plans. These plans are great places to put your "future money" because you can use pretax dollars — you pay taxes when you withdraw funds in retirement. Also, RRSP investments are often deducted from your paycheque automatically (after you request the deduction, of course!), so you won't be tempted to spend that money rather than put it away. You are allowed to put only a certain amount of your income in these types of funds, however — the Notice of Assessment from your last year's tax return will tell you how much you can put in this year — so you should look to other types of investments as well.

TFSAs

Canada Revenue Agency (CRA) gave us all a little gift recently in the form of the new Tax-Free Savings Account. As of January 2009, you can shelter up to $5,000 a year in investments in a TFSA. Although you won't get a tax deduction for the money you invest, as you would with an RRSP, you can withdraw money from your TFSA tax-free at any time and then replace it the following year. That flexibility makes the TFSA a valuable tool for retirement planning.

Mutual funds

A mutual fund pools your money with that of the other investors in the fund and then invests the money on behalf of all the investors. Mutual funds spread out the risk by investing in many companies, stocks, bonds, GICs, and other instruments.

The good thing about mutual funds is that they lower your risk. First, they're managed by professionals, who presumably are able to make wiser investment choices. Second, they invest in a range of stocks, bonds, and other vehicles (a process known as *diversification*), which means that poor performance of some elements can be offset by the good performance of others.

As a general rule, mutual funds are not appropriate for an investment of less than two years because your return will not cover the fees that you pay.

Choosing a mutual fund may seem daunting, because thousands are available. You can narrow down the possibilities by answering the following questions:

- What is your risk-tolerance factor? (See the section Identifying Your Saving and Investing Personality, at the beginning of this chapter, if you need help answering this question.) Some funds are "safer," and some take bigger risks in hopes of higher returns.
- Do you want income from your investments, or do you want your earnings to be rolled over for further investment? Choose the appropriate type of account for your needs:
  - **A dividend fund** is for people who need income to live on.
  - **All other mutual funds** are for people who are trying to maximize the size of their accounts by reinvesting their earnings.
- Do you want to invest in domestic, foreign, or mixed companies? Different funds specialize in different types of companies.
- Do you want to pay your management costs when you invest or when you withdraw from the fund?

As you narrow your choices, you'll think of other questions that will guide you to finding the right fund for you.

After you narrow down your list of prospective funds to a manageable number, investigate the fund's track record. The fund manager is the person who chooses the fund's investments, so you want to know that she or he has invested successfully in the past.

You should also be asking about the fees you pay for the fund, since those fees can eat up your profits quickly, particularly in years of low returns.

Analyzing Which Instrument Is Best for You

In choosing a savings or investment instrument, you need to match your goals and your comfort level with three factors. Those three factors are:

- The interest rate earned
- The time frame in which you want to reach your goal(s)
- The fees, penalties, and other costs associated with the investment

Interest rates, also known as *rates of return* or *ROR*, are never confusing. When you're receiving interest, you want the highest rate you can get. If the interest is compounded, you want it to be compounded (or "rolled over") in the smallest time increments possible because that's how your money grows the fastest. Simple interest is the least desirable; continuous compounding is the most desirable.

The time frame is a little bit trickier. For short-term goals, such as saving money for a new car or a new baby, you want to be able to convert your investment into cash easily and in a short time. You miss the advantages of compounding interest, but you also miss the aggravation of inflating prices. You could invest in 6-month, 9-month, or 12-month GICs, for example. These investments will earn interest for you, and thus grow, while you wait for the date of your goal.

The longer you commit to an investment, the larger the guaranteed interest rate usually is. An investment of $1,000 in a 1-year

GIC may have an annual interest rate of 2 percent, while a 5-year GIC purchased at the same time may have an annual interest rate of 3.5 percent. (To compare current rates, check out http://money. canoe.ca/rates /en/gics.html.)

For longer-term goals, you can afford a bit more fluctuation. Depending on your needs, you might choose a range of stocks or, if you're not comfortable with that level of risk, invest money in a mutual fund, which offers greater diversification and takes the everyday investment decision-making out of your hands. Of course, you still need to keep an eye on your investment to ensure you reach your goals.

When choosing savings and investment instruments, carefully read the information about fees. Doing so is even more crucial when you're just starting out. If a fund has a fixed fee of $50 and you're investing $100,000, the fee is a small price to pay for doing business with that fund (0.05 percent). If you're investing only $1,000, however, $50 is a substantial bite out of your dollars (5 percent).

Never make assumptions about the terms of any of your savings or investment instruments. If changes are made to one of your instruments, read the new terms and then keep the notices on file.

Investing Your Money: The Earlier the Better

Learning about compounding shows you the benefits of starting a savings and investment plan early. Because you earn interest now on the interest already earned, your income multiplies faster. Compounded interest is one of the reasons that putting yourself on a tight budget early in your income-earning years pays off later.

Although the amount that you regularly add to your investment fund may decrease as you pay for a house, raise children, seek more education, care for your parents, and so on, the money that you put in earlier is still growing. Table 7-1 shows the consequences of your decision on when to start saving and investing.

Table 7-1: The Timing of Your Investment Influences Your Return

Mary Anne				Karl			
Age	Years	Contributions	End-of-Year Value	Age	Years	Contributions	End-of-Year Value
25	1	$2,000	$2,145	25	1	$0	$0
26	2	$2,000	$4,444	26	2	$0	$0
27	3	$2,000	$6,910	27	3	$0	$0
28	4	$2,000	$9,554	28	4	$0	$0
29	5	$2,000	$12,389	29	5	$0	$0
30	6	$2,000	$15,430	30	6	$0	$0
31	7	$2,000	$18,680	31	7	$0	$0
32	8	$2,000	$22,185	32	8	$0	$0
33	9	$2,000	$25,934	33	9	$0	$0
34	10	$2,000	$29,953	34	10	$0	$0
35	11	$0	$32,118	35	11	$2,000	$2,145
36	12	$0	$34,440	36	12	$2,000	$4,445
37	13	$0	$36,930	37	13	$2,000	$6,910
38	14	$0	$39,598	38	14	$2,000	$9,554
39	15	$0	$42,462	39	15	$2,000	$12,390
40	16	$0	$45,532	40	16	$2,000	$15,430
41	17	$0	$48,823	41	17	$2,000	$18,690
42	18	$0	$52,353	42	18	$2,000	$22,185
43	19	$0	$56,137	43	19	$2,000	$25,934
44	20	$0	$60,195	44	20	$2,000	$29,953
45	21	$0	$64,547	45	21	$2,000	$34,263
46	22	$0	$69,213	46	22	$2,000	$38,884

continued

Mary Anne				Karl			
Age	Years	Contri-butions	End-of-Year Value	Age	Years	Contri-butions	End-of-Year Value
47	23	$0	$74,216	47	23	$2,000	$43,840
48	24	$0	$79,582	48	24	$2,000	$49,154
49	25	$0	$85,334	49	25	$2,000	$54,851
50	26	$0	$91,503	50	26	$2,000	$60,961
51	27	$0	$98,118	51	27	$2,000	$67,513
52	28	$0	$105,221	52	28	$2,000	$74,538
53	29	$0	$112,817	53	29	$2,000	$82,070
54	30	$0	$120,972	54	30	$2,000	$90,148
55	31	$0	$129,717	55	31	$2,000	$98,810
56	32	$0	$139,094	56	32	$2,000	$108,097
57	33	$0	$149,150	57	33	$2,000	$118,056
58	34	$0	$159,932	58	34	$2,000	$128,735
59	35	$0	$171,493	59	35	$2,000	$140,187
60	36	$0	$183,890	60	36	$2,000	$152,464
61	37	$0	$197,184	61	37	$2,000	$165,631
62	38	$0	$211,438	62	38	$2,000	$179,749
63	39	$0	$226,723	63	39	$2,000	$194,887
64	40	$0	$243,113	64	40	$2,000	$211,121
65	41	$0	$260,690	65	41	$2,000	$228,530
Value at retirement: $260,690				Value at retirement: $228,530			
Minus total contributions: $20,000				Minus total contributions: $62,000			
Net earnings: $240,690				Net earnings: $166,530			

By waiting 10 years, Karl had to put in more than three times as much money as Mary Anne, and he still held an investment worth almost 12 percent less than hers. When they turned 65, Mary Anne's investment had increased by $17,577 the preceding year, even though she added nothing to her fund.

Karl's fund increased by $17,409, but he added $2,000 to it during that year.

Even if you're not as young as Karl and Mary Anne when you start investing, the younger you are, the more money you'll have when you retire, and the less money will have to come out of your paycheque.

The return you earn on your investment makes a big difference to how fast your money grows. The above chart assumes a 7 percent return on investment per year. In today's low-interest rate environment, you would have to look toward equity investments to earn that much on your investments annually. Keep in mind, however, that equity investments can actually depreciate in value, unlike fixed income investments like GICs. It's in your interest to try to balance investment risk against the potential for higher returns.

If you don't want to spend your life researching and making decisions about your investments, a mutual fund that reinvests dividends may be the best choice for you. Because you'll never see a cheque for what your investment earns, you won't be tempted to divert it from your retirement funding.

Tracking Your Investments

Tracking is keeping records of how each of your investments is performing. Tracking may take a variety of forms, from simple lists to charts and graphs. People learn in different ways, so choose the form that makes it easiest for you to get quick and clear answers to your questions.

You can use a simple form like the following worksheet to track the performance of your mutual fund investments. You can use this information elsewhere to figure your gains (or losses) as adjusted for inflation, taxes, and so on (although this example makes no such adjustments).

My Mutual Fund Record

Date: _____

Fund name: _____

Fund manager: _____

Fund type: _____

Date purchased: _____

Number of shares purchased: _____

Purchase price per share: _____

Total cost: _____

Date shares reinvested: _____

Current number of shares: _____

Current price per share: _____

Current value: _____

Dividend paid: _____

Date sold: _____

Number of shares sold: _____

Money received: _____

Profit (Loss): _____

Total annual management fees: _____

Keep the same kind of record for your stock investments. The following worksheet shows you how to record information that's appropriate to stock purchases and sales.

My Stock Record

Date: _____

Stock name: _____

Date purchased: _____

Number of shares purchased: _____

Price per share: _____

Total cost: _____

Stock split date: _____

Current number of shares: _____

Current price per share: _____

Current value: _____

Date sold: _____

Number of shares sold: _____

Money received: _____

Profit (Loss): _____

Perhaps you decided to invest in bonds. The information you need to record is slightly different, as shown in the following worksheet.

My Bond Record

Date: _____

Name of bond: _____

Bond number or book entry number: _____

Bond type: _____

Bond price: _____

Date of purchase: _____

Sale/Maturity date: _____

Current interest yield: _____

Tax status: _____

Conversion callable features: _____

Net sales price: _____

Net gain/loss: _____

If a bond is called, it stops earning interest on the call date. Make sure to redeem called bonds by the call date.

If you use a personal accounting software package such as Quicken, then keeping track of your investments is even easier. Some of the available features are:

- The ability to track individual investments
- The ability to keep track of entire portfolios
- Graphs showing the history of each of your investments
- Registers showing every transaction for a portfolio

You can create any of these categories on paper, but the software makes record-keeping much easier. For example, you can update your Share Balance or Cash Balance records. Instead of having to create a transaction to reflect the new number of shares held, you can make these adjustments directly on the balance sheet.

Investment reports help you see the trends in how your investments are performing. Some of the reports you can create are:

- Capital gains
- Investment income
- Investment transactions
- The value of your portfolio

Using financial software you can create pie charts that make it easy to compare how parts of your portfolio are performing. For example, you can create two pie charts showing what percentages of your portfolio are invested in low-risk, medium-risk, and high-risk investments, side by side with a pie chart showing what percentage of your total income each of those groups contributed. Having this picture of investments and returns together helps you decide where you want to distribute your investment dollars in the future.

Quicken offers its own Mutual Fund Finder. You can choose criteria based on the investment questions that you answered earlier in this chapter. After you decide what you want from your investment instrument, the Mutual Fund Finder lists those funds that meet your needs. You can even rank funds so that the information is in an even more useful form.

The Internet is a great source of data on which to make your decisions. You can download financial news, price updates for instruments in your portfolio, and historical data about your stocks (or ones that you're interested in buying). Websites like www. morningstar.ca and fundlibrary.com provide detailed information on Canadian mutual funds, including in-depth fund profiles, reports, news, and analysis.

Why you do it

Tracking the performance of your investments keeps you current on trends involving your own investments and in the market as a whole. Efficient investing, like budgeting, relies on good information.

In every other part of your financial planning, you consider how your decisions will affect your income tax bill. That consideration is at least as important in investing. Unlike wages, you control when you pay taxes on your investments by the types of investments you choose. Using software to insert new data and see the overall impact makes it easier to track — and makes ignoring it less acceptable.

How you do it

Probably the number one rule is to read all the information that the companies with which you hold mutual funds, stocks, and bonds send to you. Online information is fine, but the literature that you get directly from the companies contains information that, apart from finances, defines how you want to make decisions.

In addition to what comes in the mail, you can check your newspaper or the Internet to compare your fund with others. This information, in the words of musician Kenny Rogers, helps you "know when to hold 'em and know when to fold 'em."

Your comparison may take the form of a graph, pie chart, or bar chart. It can compare:

- Your stock's actual performance with its anticipated performance
- Two stocks that you own
- A stock that you bought with one that you were thinking of buying
- The performance of your stocks against an index such as the S&P/TSX composite index

Taking the time to chart these comparisons will go a long way to increasing your understanding of the hows and whys of investing.

once you've reached your first goal

IN THIS CHAPTER

- Enjoying the fruits of your victory over financial indecision
- Accounting for changes in your lifestyle and your income
- Using the reinforcement from your past fiscal victories to stay on your course of budgeting and saving

Doesn't it feel good to know where your money's going? Aren't you enjoying all the energy that you're *not* spending on worrying about money? Isn't it nice to have a picture of your financial future?

When you started on this journey, you spent a lot of time gathering information. Then you had to make decisions — a *lot* of decisions — about the information you gathered. The fact that you're now reading Chapter 8 means that you saw the value of those exercises, you did them, and you have your budget firmly in control.

But as we've emphasized earlier, a budget isn't a static thing. As you change, your needs will change, and so must your budget. This chapter talks about how to maintain and make adjustments to your budget so that you can deal with those changes.

Enjoying the Fruits of Your Frugality

If you've planned well, whatever you want is now in your budget. If you don't believe that, walk through the following process:

1. You want to take a three-week trip to Paris. You look at your budget. You have plenty of money in your savings account. Unfortunately, that's not your vacation savings account, and you don't have enough in your vacation account. You can pay for your flight to and from the City of Lights, and even a hotel. But you don't have enough left to eat, pay admission to the museums, or even ride the Metro. Realizing that you need to regroup, you go on to Step 2.

2. If you take the same amount and stay in Paris for only two weeks, you can eat and see the sights, too. You won't be able to eat well (in Paris!), and you won't be able to see all the sights, but you'll still have a nice vacation. But you wonder whether a skimpy trip without much in the way of luxuries is what you want. So you survey other choices. On to Step 3.

3. You could go to Paris for one week. Doing so would move enough money from your hotel fund to your food and entertainment fund to give you a first-class vacation. One drawback is that the transportation time and cost are the same whether you stay for one week or three. Keeping a one-week trip as an option, you go on to Step 4.

4. Looking closer to home, you find Montreal. They speak French there. They have museums. They have great restaurants. Your cousin Fred will put you up for your stay.

You now have two alternatives that can meet at least part of your goal. No robbing Peter to pay Paul. No borrowing from your long-term savings for a short-term treat. No stress. And you still get to choose between one week in Paris and three weeks in Montreal.

This is just one simple example of how you should be making financial decisions now. Every choice has a benefit, and you know what that benefit is. Every choice has a negative side, too, and you are aware of that side as well. After finishing all those surveys about your financial picture and making all those choices based on your personal alternatives, good financial decisions are now at your fingertips.

Rebudgeting for Change

Where does rebudgeting come in? You choose to change your budget either when you're financially uncomfortable or when a major change in your life affects your financial situation. (The vacation example is not a case of rebudgeting; it's a reallocation of funds that you've already budgeted.)

What should I do with that raise?

You got a raise, and you're going to spend it. Isn't that what a raise is for? The question is, how are you going to spend it? Review your budget to identify likely items to which you may want to apply that new money:

- Buy new furniture
- Go on vacation or upgrade your vacation
- Invest
- Pay down your mortgage early
- Pay off old debts
- Make a gift to your place of worship or alma mater
- Start an education fund for your children
- Go back to school
- Contract for a cleaning service

The last choice may have surprised you, but remember that you're not supposed to deny yourself everything. You're just supposed to make a decision about every financial move you make and be aware of the pluses and minuses of each decision.

Explore the cleaner idea, for example. Do you have a hobby that you'd like to turn into a business, but you're already working full-time? Hiring a cleaner could free enough time for you to follow your dream. Over the long term, will having a cleaner allow you to make more money than you pay for his or her services?

Or maybe you just hate cleaning. You earned the money, so you can make the decision to have the cleaning done for you if you want to. It's okay to make a decision just because it's something you want, as long as you know what alternatives you're choosing to do without.

If you use the extra money in your paycheque to pay for a short-term goal, such as buying new furniture or going on vacation, either you can decide now what you want to do with the extra money after you meet the short-term goal, or you can wait until you meet that goal and then go through the decision-making process again.

If you decide on a long-term goal, you still have decisions to make. For example, if the money is going into investments, will you choose risky or safe investments? Your previous work should have put you in good stead to make wise decisions that will lead to a stronger financial future.

What you can't do is *not* make a decision. Your money will be gone, and you either won't know where it went or you'll have buyer's remorse because you'll wish that you'd spent it on something else.

We're having a baby!

As happy as the news of a baby on the way is for couples, it's also a cause for panic among the ill-prepared. One of the first questions they may ask is, "How are we going to pay for this?"

Even if the baby is a surprise, you're prepared to reorganize your funds and reprioritize your goals quickly because you have a budget and a savings plan. You know where all your money is going, and you've identified opportunities for cutting more spending or earning extra income. Therefore, you have everything you need to make a good decision about reallocating your funds to meet your new obligations.

Having a baby is more than just hugs and diapers. Using the evaluation skills that you've developed by reading this book, you need to make decisions about other changes, such as:

- Do you need more insurance?
- Do you need larger housing? If not now, when in the future?
- How are you going to pay for the ongoing costs of diapers, clothing, food, health care, child care, schooling, summer camps, sports, high school formals, weddings, and all the rest?

And what a lucky baby! From her first allowance, you'll be teaching her the same good money-managing skills that you've learned.

Let's buy a house!

The time has come. You set up a fund to save for a down payment on a home. You decided how much you can afford to pay for your new home, so you've already saved a 25 percent down payment, which means you don't have to buy expensive mortgage insurance. Now you get to make specific decisions about where you'll live.

Review your goals now. List what you want:

- Specific neighbourhood or type of neighbourhood
- Number of bedrooms
- Number of bathrooms
- Style: Victorian, modern, something else
- Number of levels: one, two, or more
- Garage and/or size of garage
- Yard specifications
- Distance from schools
- Kitchen specifications
- Living and dining room specifications
- Other specific rooms, like an office, library, or pantry
- Amenities, such as central air conditioning or a security system

Any real estate office will have forms to help you decide what you want in a house. Your local library and online sources should also have plenty of information about home buying.

The best-laid plans will go awry. As a good/bad example: Marie got the house she wanted when the previous buyers backed out. They wanted to use the finished basement as a den. The problem was that their furniture was too tall to go down the basement stairs. Investigate *everything* about your purchase. Be flexible. Be prepared.

The down payment is only the first piece of the buying puzzle. To avoid unpleasant financial surprises, you also need to make sure that you have enough money to cover:

- Moving expenses
- Points and other closing costs paid to the lender and due at closing
- Redecorating and/or repair expenses
- Monthly mortgage payments
- Property taxes
- Homeowner's insurance

Saving money is a foundation of budgeting and having a savings/financial plan. If you concentrate too much on the dollar sign and not enough on quality, however, you could be in for some nasty financial surprises. This doesn't mean that you need to pay top dollar, but asking others for recommendations can help you stay out of the quicksand.

Areas in which you should shop for bargains but be very careful in your choices are the following:

- Movers. (Get recommendations from people who have been happy with their movers.)
- Painting and decorating supplies. (Applying bad paint takes the same amount of time and energy as applying good paint.)

- Cleaning supplies. (Paying more doesn't mean that the product cleans better.)
- Packing materials. (Skimping here will lead to breakage.)
- Appliances. (If you don't have all the appliances you need, figure out what you can do without for the time being so that you can buy the best quality for your current needs.)

Retaining Your Good Habits

The Introduction to this book promised you that if you gathered the information required and made step-by-step decisions, the end result would be a financial plan that enables you to reach your short-term, mid-term, and long-term goals.

Because you're reading this section, we know that you followed the plan. You recognize that the steps you took have constructed a sound, firm financial plan. This is a good time to review all your "homework." To keep up your good habits, review your budget, your investment records, your net worth statement, and your personal property inventory.

Did you find that this review offered any real surprises? Probably not. You've been using these records all along. What you should do is appreciate how much in-depth knowledge you have about your financial affairs. That hard data, along with your knowledge of your saving and spending personalities, gives you the background to make future decisions without having to go through the entire process again. You get to enjoy the time you save and the stress you avoid.

Knowing the advantages that you've gained from your previous work ensures that you'll continue using the process outlined in this book to keep your financial records up to date.

What changes can you expect? As you move through life, you'll meet your short-term goals, and what were mid-term goals will become short-term goals. As you recognize your spending personality and make choices that make the most of your strengths and accommodate your weaknesses, your spending personality itself will evolve. Recognizing those changes, you'll want to re-evaluate your spending personality periodically so that you can base future decisions on current information.

Likewise, your saving and investing personality will change. Part of the change will come because, as you age and either meet or fail to meet your goals, the way you feel about saving and investing will change. Revisit the section in Chapter 7 on recognizing your saving personality and redefine your saving personality so that you can base future decisions on your updated profile.

You know how difficult breaking a bad habit can be. Every time you go back to the bad habit, that habit becomes even stronger.

Luckily, the same is true of good habits. Take a minute to think of a good habit that you exercise without even thinking about it. For example, you may never litter because you were taught not to litter when you were very young. Do you say "Please" and "Thank you"? You probably don't even think of these things or give yourself credit for them.

The habit of following the financial planning habits and spending decision habits that you learned from this book will become stronger and stronger as you practise it. If you give yourself credit for all that you've accomplished, you'll want to continue those good habits.

final review

Use this Final Review to practise what you've learned in this book and to build your confidence in doing the job right the first time. After you work through the review questions, the problem-solving exercises, and the fun and useful scenarios and Practice Project, you're well on your way to achieving your goal of creating and using a budget.

Q&A

1. What is compounding?

    a. The accrual of interest on a debt
    b. Interest paid on interest
    c. The complicated nature of budgeting

2. You can do your banking online.

   True
   or
   False

3. Fixed expenses include:

   a. Health care, housing, and insurance
   b. Housing, food, and entertainment
   c. Clothing, movies, and CDs

4. List three good financial habits that you have already
   established.

   1. _____

      _____

      _____

      _____

   2. _____

      _____

      _____

      _____

   3. _____

      _____

      _____

      _____

5. Name your most common spending trigger.

_____

_____

_____

_____

_____

_____

_____

_____

_____

_____

_____

_____

_____

_____

_____

_____

_____

_____

_____

_____

_____

_____

_____

_____

6. You should buy an item if you have a coupon for it, whether or not you really need it.

   True
   or
   False

7. The following is a good way to live on less:

   a. Stop eating breakfast every day
   b. Buy a bagel and a cup of gourmet coffee on your way to work
   c. Take your lunch to work rather than go out to eat

8. When you're in debt, your best bet is to:

   a. Continue using your credit cards, even if you're already carrying a balance
   b. Borrow money from your friends
   c. Pay off your highest-interest debts first

9. Name three future goals that you may need to rebudget for.

1. _____
   _____
   _____
   _____
   _____
   _____
   _____

2. _____
   _____
   _____
   _____
   _____
   _____
   _____

3. _____
   _____
   _____
   _____
   _____
   _____
   _____

Scenario

You decide that you want to purchase a new car in one year. To ensure that you have enough money for a down payment, you should

Answers

Q&A Answers
1. b
2. True
3. a
4. Answers will vary
5. Answers will vary
6. False
7. c
8. c
9. Answers will vary

Scenario Answer
Figure out how much you need to save per month for the down payment, and then add that amount as a fixed expense in your budget.

Consider This

- Did you know that little purchases that you don't even think about can do the worst damage to your budget? See Chapter 2 for more information.
- Did you know that you can rack up a lot of debt quickly by using credit cards and not paying off the balances each month? See Chapter 6 to find out how to tackle your debt.
- Did you know that you can buy anything you want if you just put it into your budget and have the patience to save up the money you need? See Chapter 3 for instructions for creating a budget, and Chapter 4 for tips on how to stick to it.

Practice Project

1. Track your spending on food, including snacks and soft drinks from vending machines, for one week. For tips on tracking your spending, see Chapter 2.
2. At the end of the week, identify which expenditures you could have done without, and tally how much those expenditures cost.
3. Make a list of the goals you could have come closer to achieving by putting this money toward them rather than spending it on junk food, gourmet coffee, and the like.
4. Remember this exercise the next time you're about to make a purchase without thinking about the financial consequences of it!

resource centre

Internet
Check out these websites for more information about mastering your budgeting and financial life:

Canoe
money.canoe.ca. Canoe Money offers scads of financial information, with an emphasis on business-related news stories from wire services. Also has personal finance tools, like a glossary of financial terms and a mortgage calculator, as well as a mutual fund tracker.

MSN Money
money.ca.msn.com. MSN's personal finance site offers advice on retirement planning, taxes, estate planning, buying a home, and purchasing insurance, among other helpful features.

Debt-Proof Living Online

debtproofliving.com. This site is packed with tips for tightening your belt, so to speak, and can help you stick to your cost-saving ways.

Moneyminded

moneyminded.com. Primarily women-centred, this site has advice that is on-target for anyone. It offers information about everything from budgets to money personality to spending habits to investing.

GlobeInvestor

globeinvestor.com. The financial site of the national newspaper *The Globe and Mail*, GlobeInvestor is a thorough page whose strong point is business news from the paper and wire services, as well as stock quotes.

Morningstar

www.morningstar.ca and Fund Library, fundlibrary.com. These sites offer in-depth fund profiles, as well as reports, news, and analysis. You can see at a glance how your fund has performed compared to benchmark stock market indices, or compare your fund to similar funds.

Magazines

Try the following publications for additional, current information about the world of personal finance:

Canadian Business, Financial Post Magazine, Report on Business Magazine: Canada's three leading business publications — the latter two of which are published by the two national newspapers — are generally geared to financial and business professionals; however, they often feature advice on personal investing and financial planning, too.

notes

notes

notes